Featured Artists

1. Nancy Sutton Lewin
2. Linda Fauconnier (Lilly. F. T)
3. T.J.
4. Arianne Schimmel
5. Jeanne Burbage
6. Maud Feral-Chauveau
7. Jovian Ko
8. Nancy43
9. Debbie Lai
10. Rover Hsiao

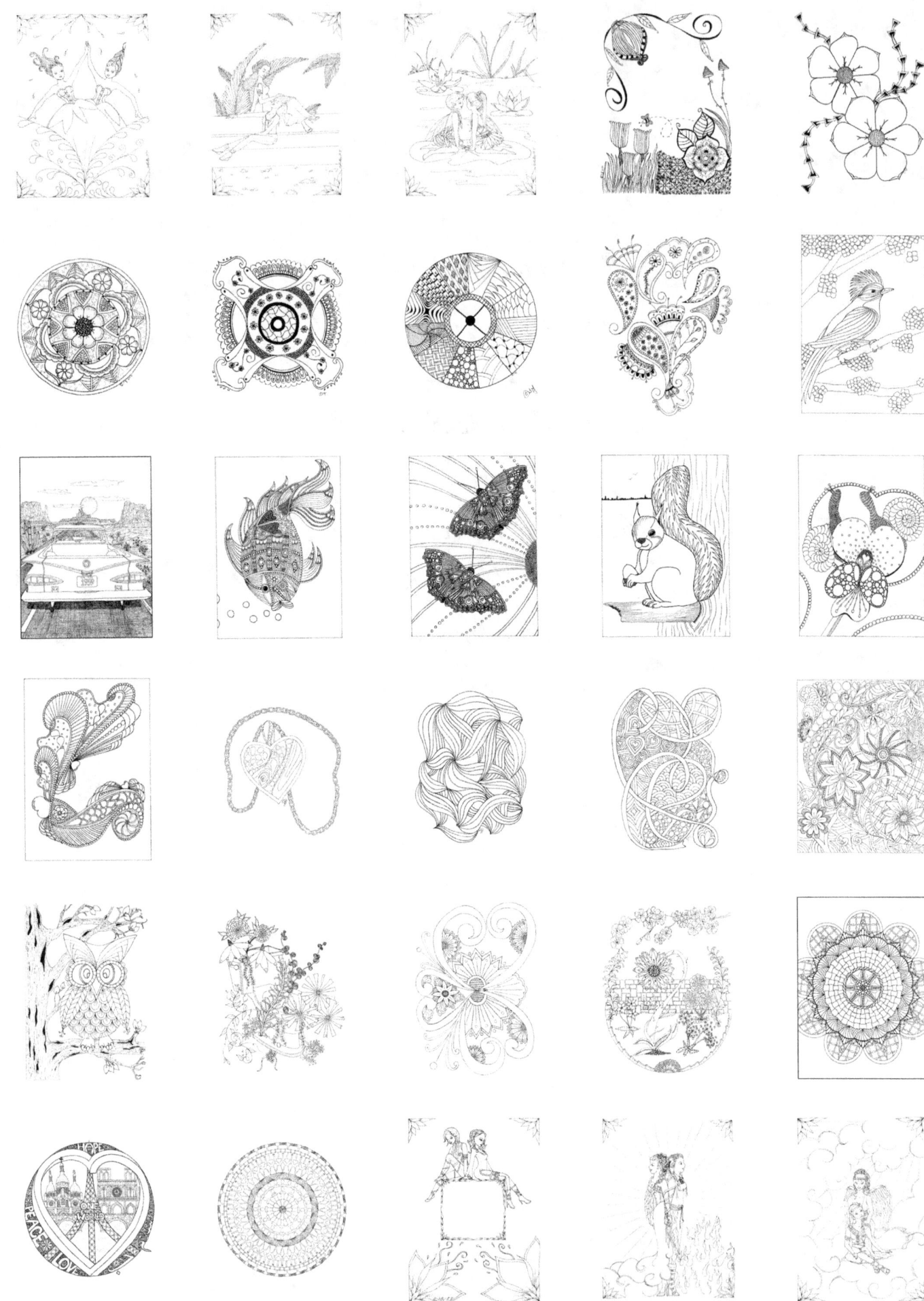

Drawn & colored by Arianne Schimmel

Drawn by Maud Feral & colored by Amandine

Global Doodle Gems Volume 18
"The Ultimate International Coloring Book...an epic Collection from Artists around the World!"

Drawn & colored by Nancy Sutton Lewin

Drawn & colored by Nancy43

Drawn & colored by TJ

Drawn by Debbie Lai & colored by Jenny Wei

Drawn & colored by Jeanne Burbage

Drawn & colored by Rover Hsiao

Drawn & colored by Linda F. Tricoire

Drawn & colored by Jovian Ko

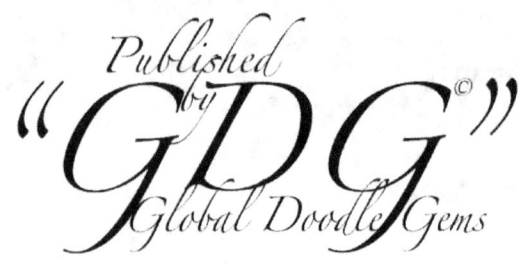

Share your colored versions with us ! We love seeing your results and hearing from you we are social !

The Official FB book page, stay on top of what we have in the works !
www.facebook.com/globaldoodlegems
The Community group, share your colored pages, meet the artists, enjoy exclusive freebies, take part in community Charity books and so much more......
www.facebook.com/groups/globaldoodlegems/
Follow us on Twitter.... @GlobalDoodlegem
We are on Instagram too
@globaldoodlegems for instagram
...and if you are not social like that we have a blog
globaldoodlegems.wordpress.com

Copyright © 2017 Global Doodle Gems
All rights are reserved by Global Doodle Gems.
Duplication of pages for personal use are allowed. You are invited to color the pages then scan/post your coloured versions to social networks, mentioning the book title and author/artist (Global Doodle Gems).
All artwork and images are protected by copyright laws. This book or any portion thereof may not, otherwise, be reproduced and/or distributed or transmitted without the express written permission of the artist/publisher of Global Doodle Gems.
All of us from the Global Doodle Gems wish you a colortastic time and look forward to seeing your wonderful color results online !

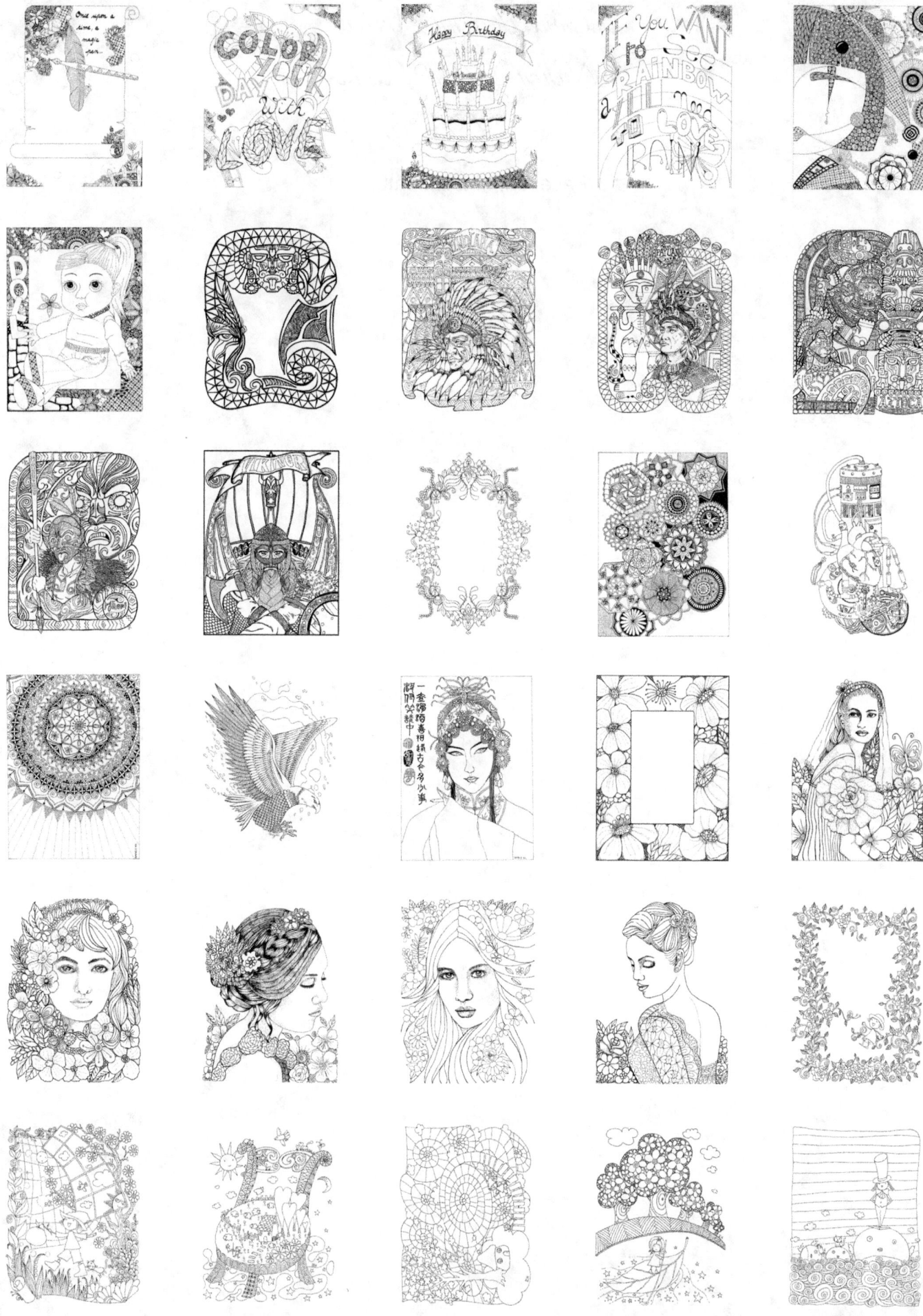

Contributing Artist
Nancy Sutton Lewin
USA

Facebook :Iridescentbug

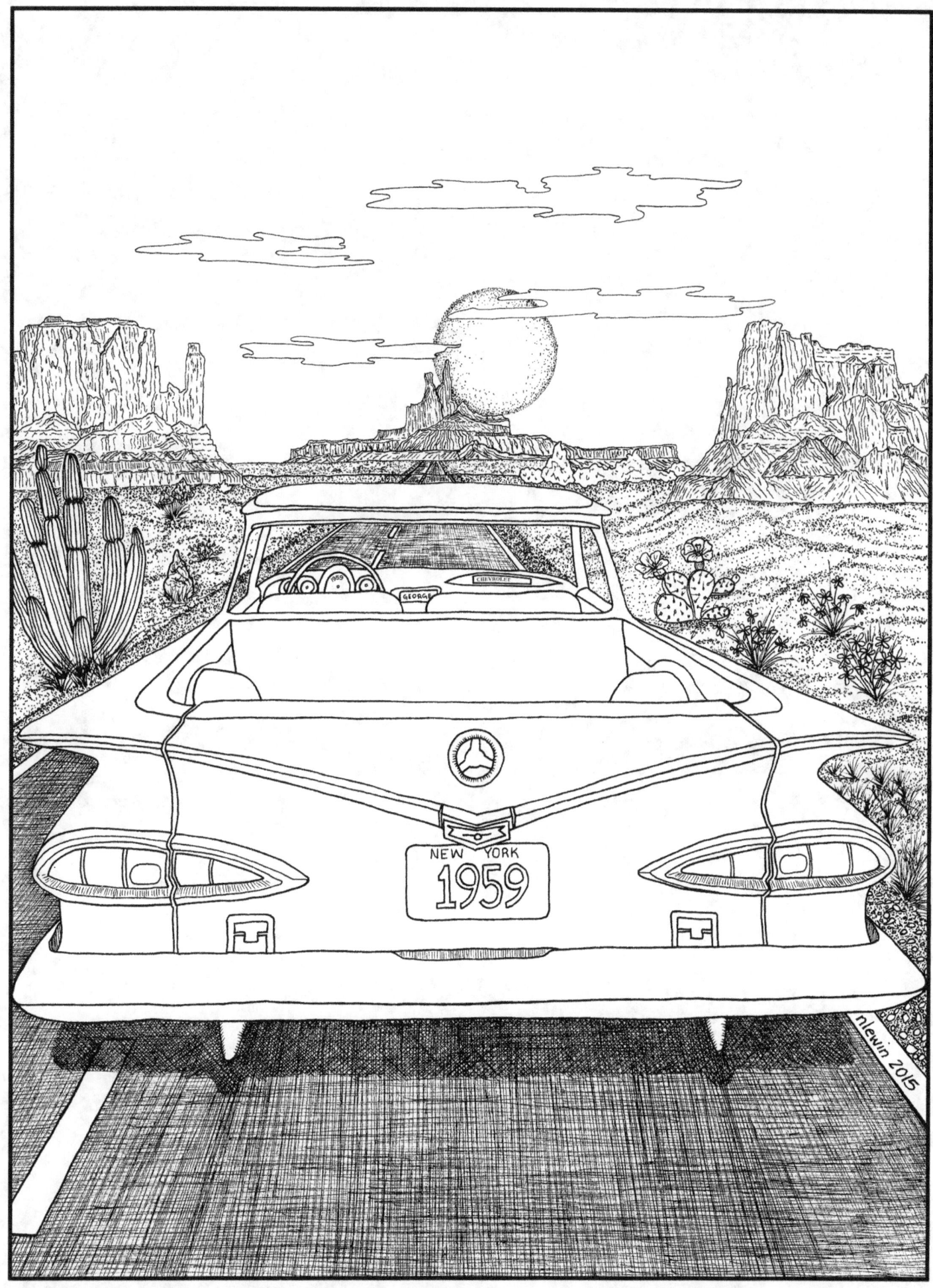

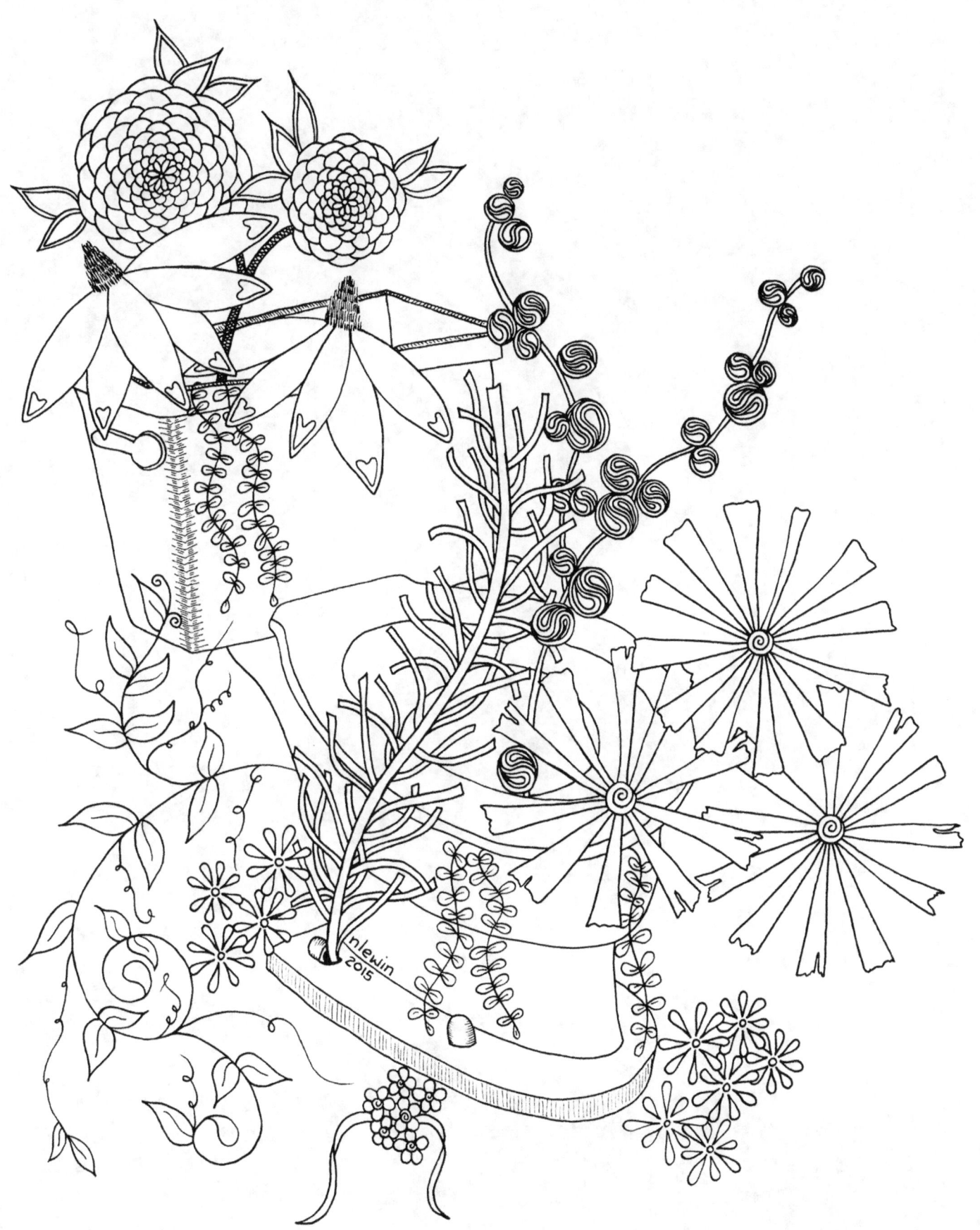

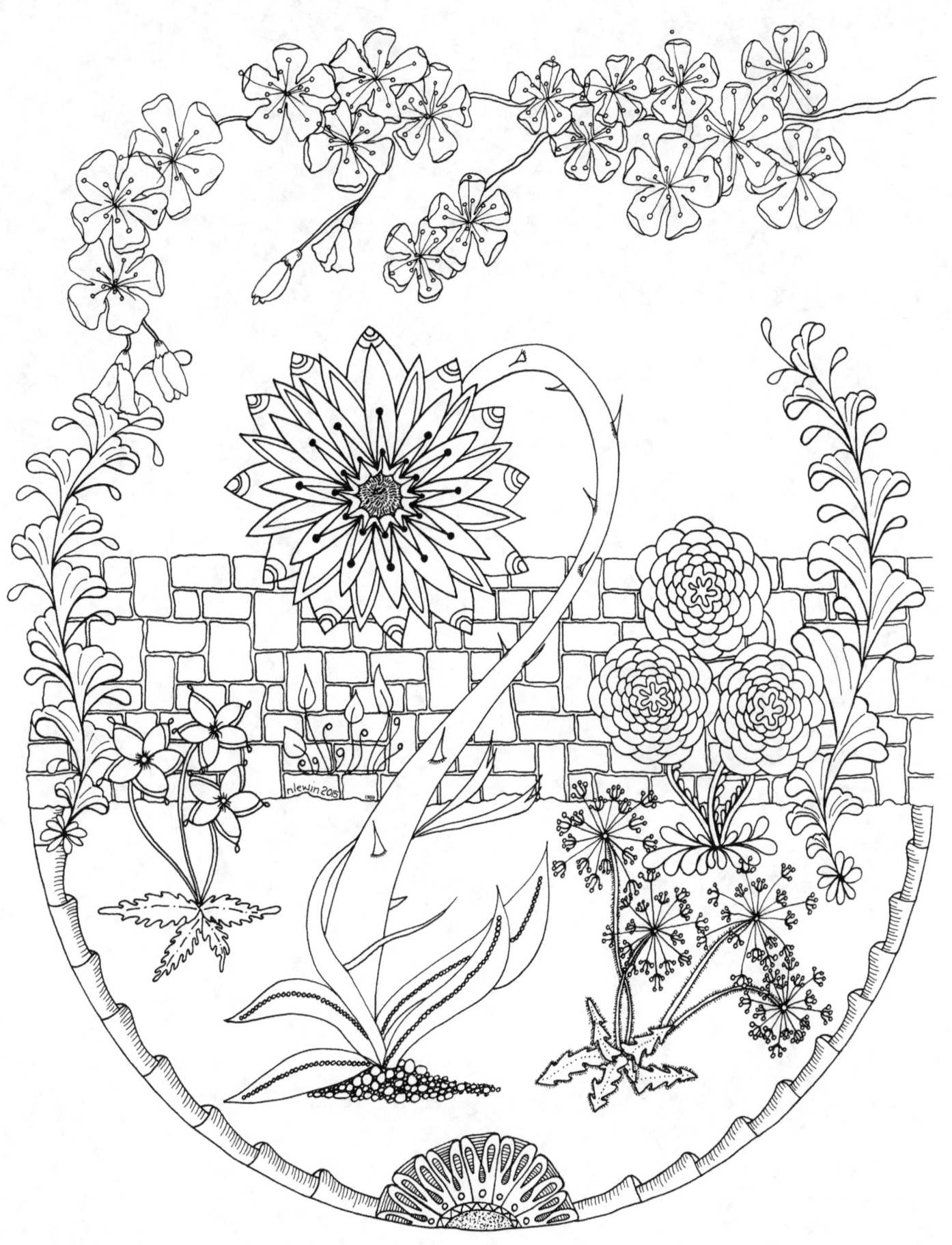

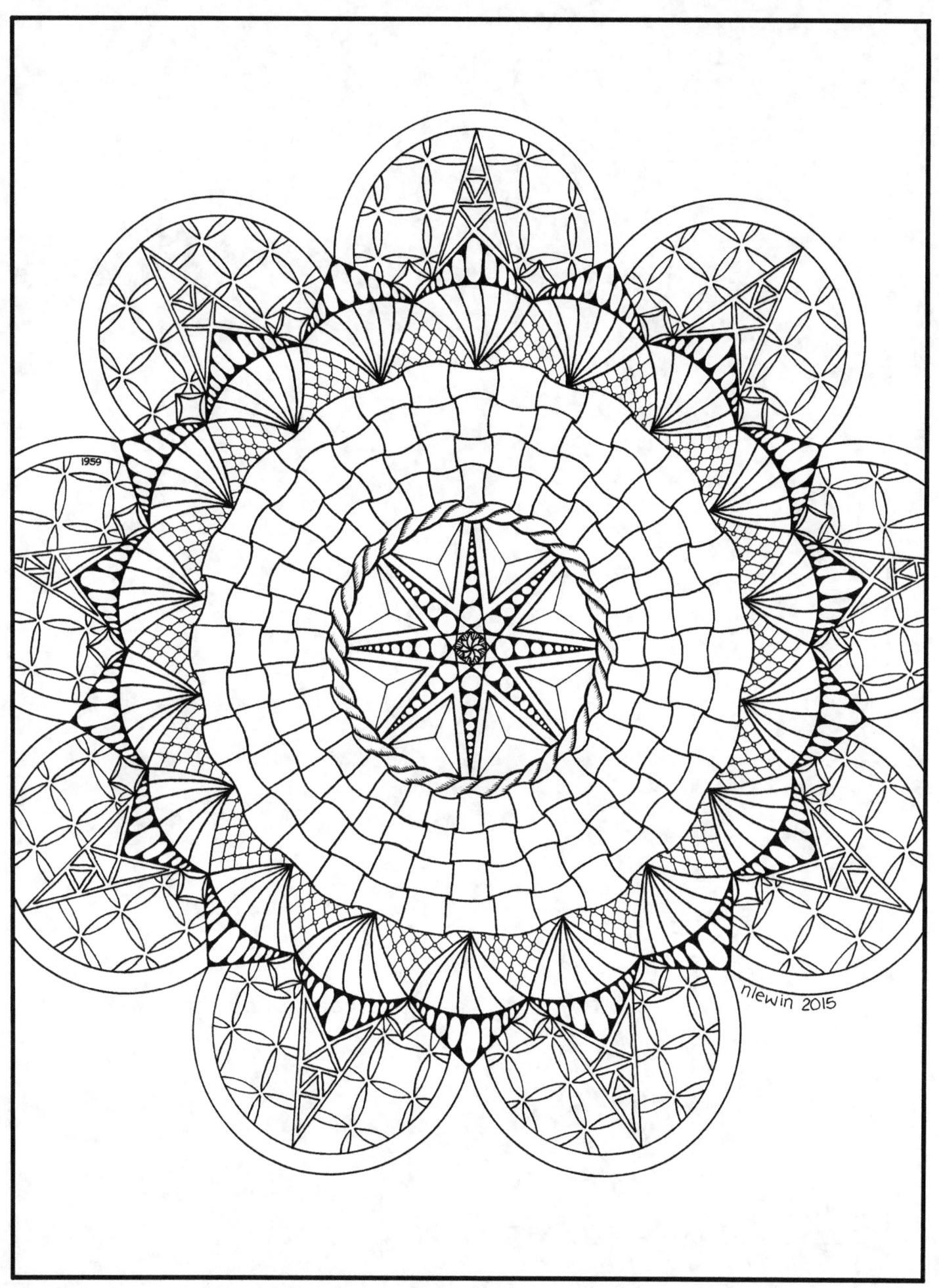

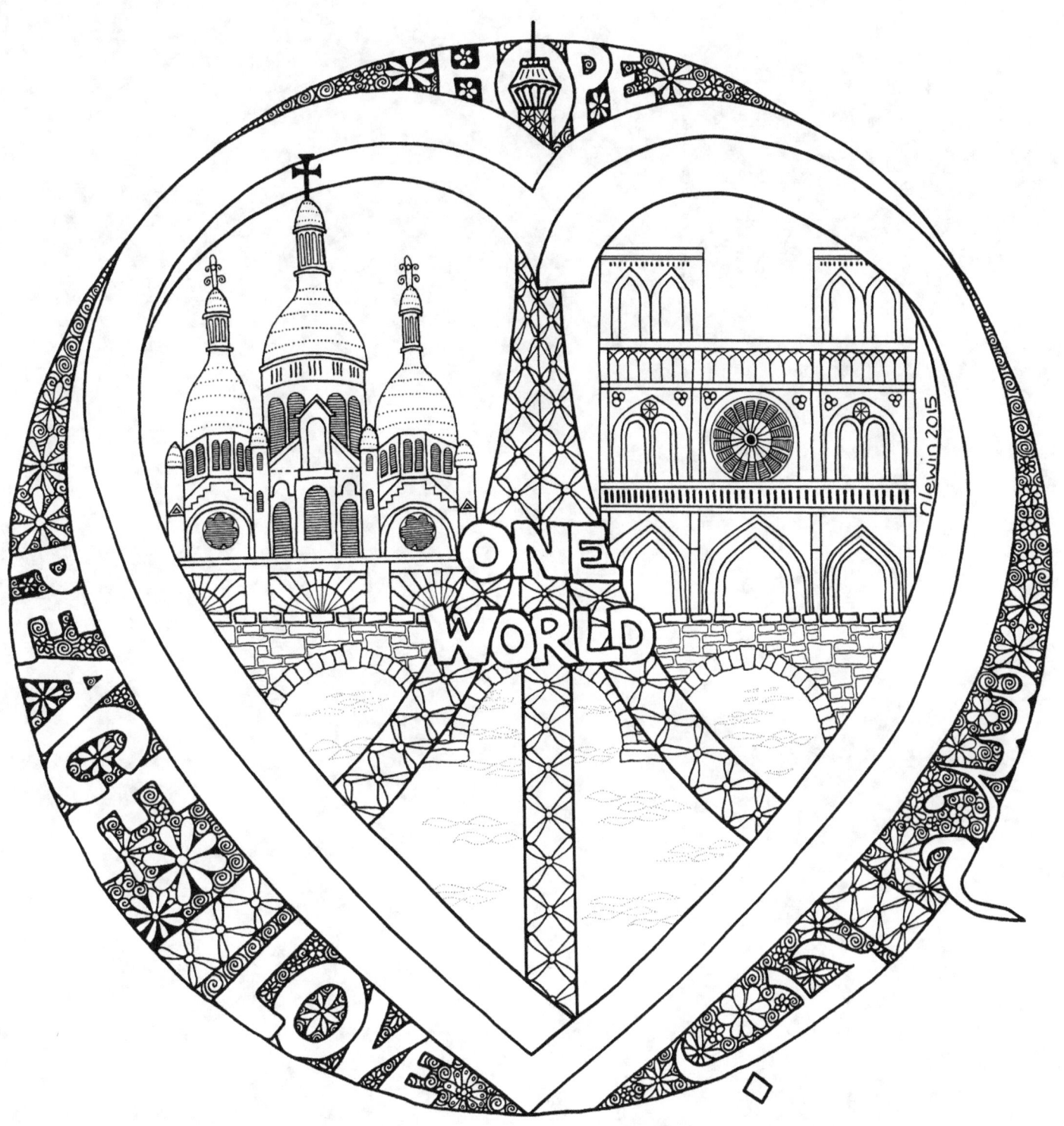

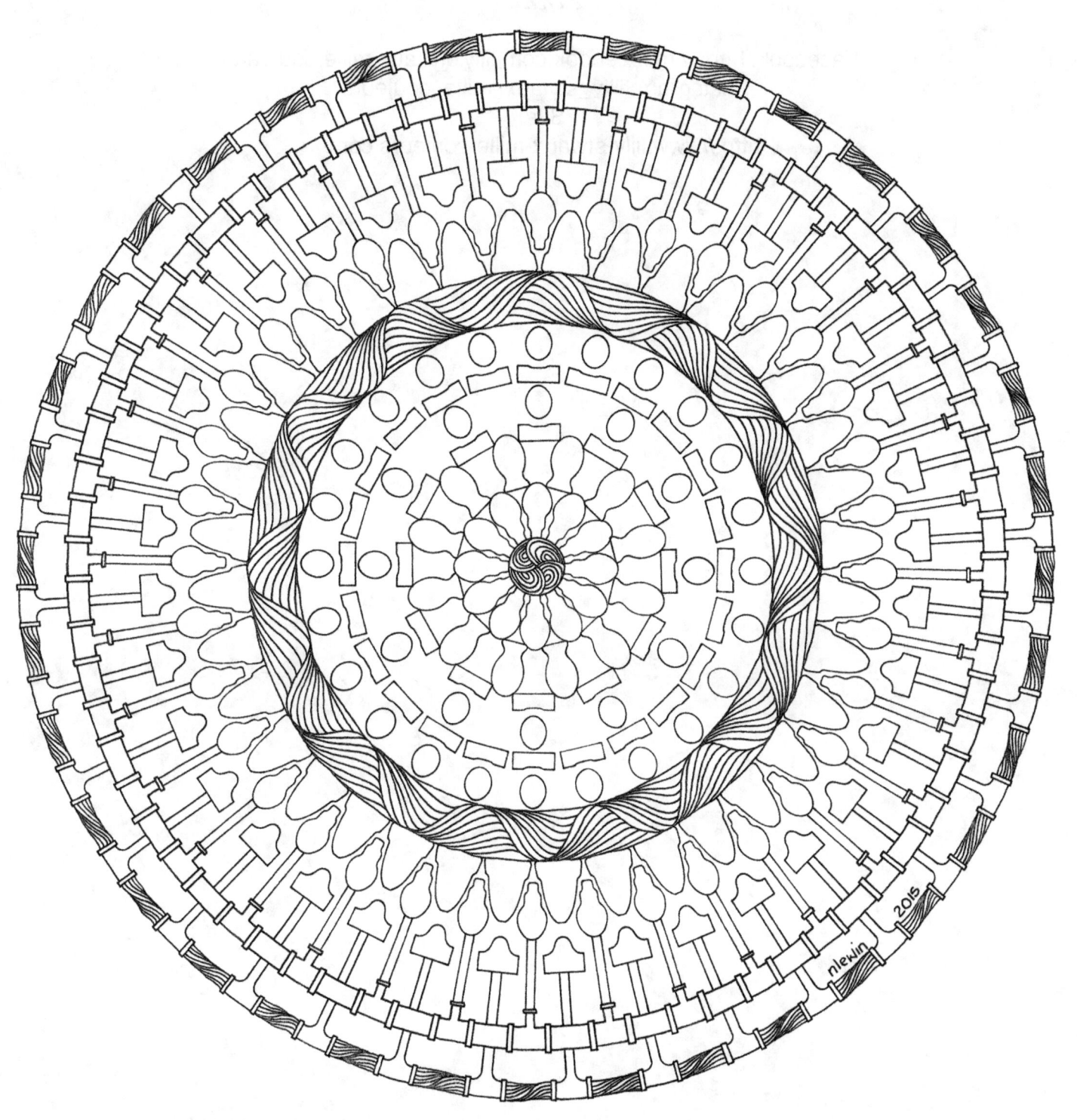

Contributing Artist
Linda Fauconnier (Lilly. F. T)
France

Facebook: https://m.facebook.com/lilly.styl.aux.mille.couleurs/
Instagram: lilly_stylaux_mille_couleurs
Site:
http://www.lilly-stylaux-mille-couleurs.com/

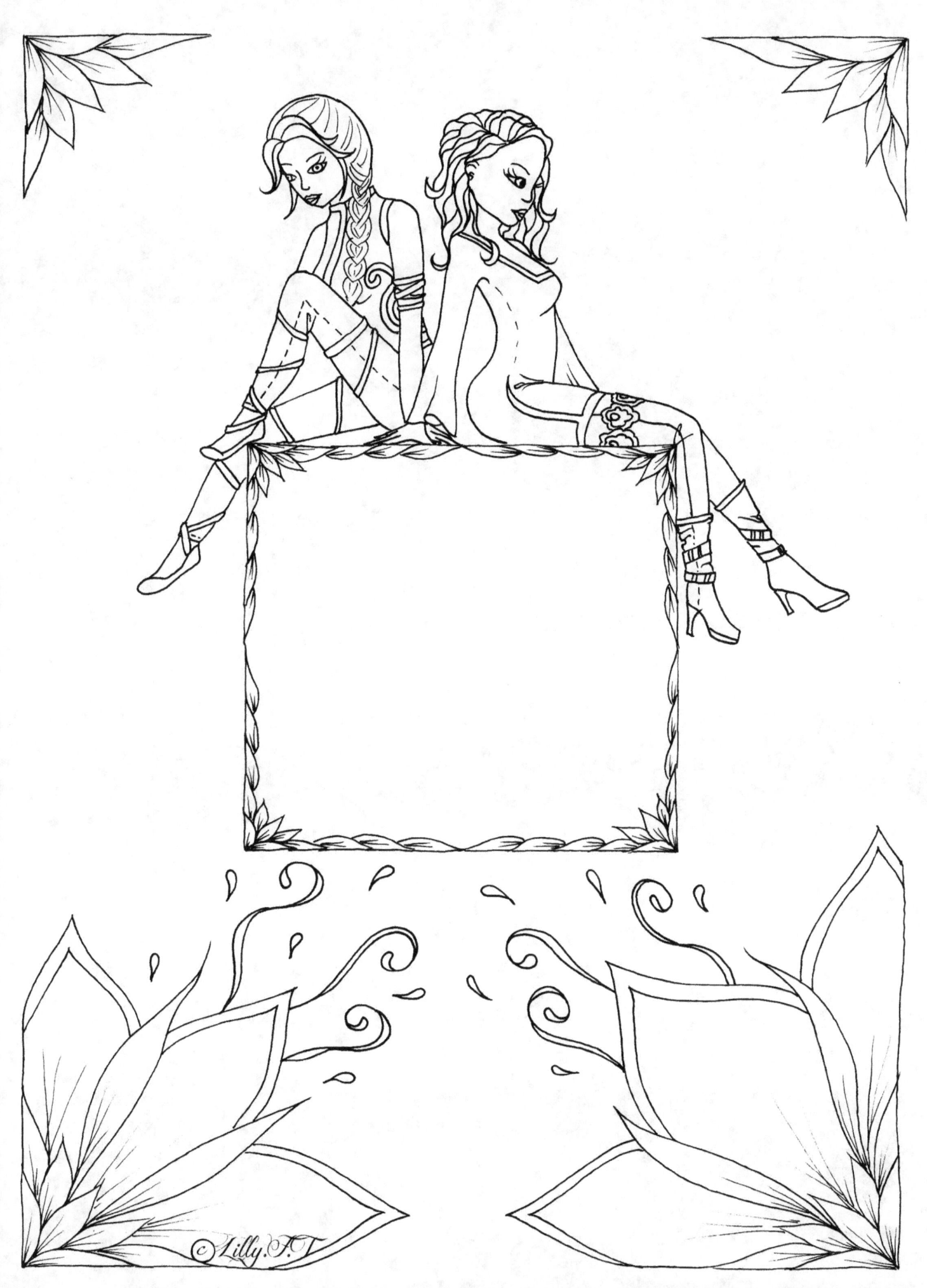

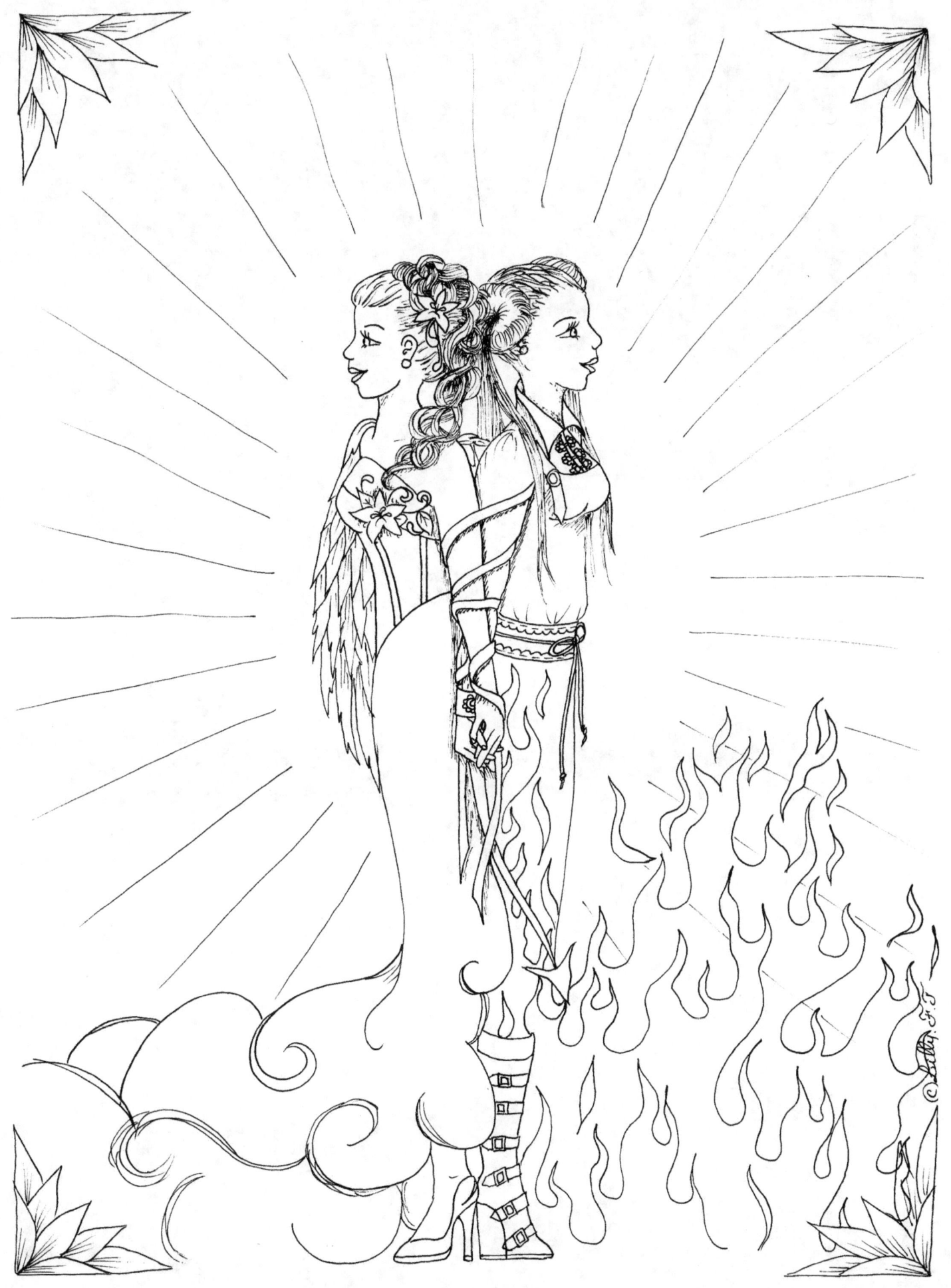

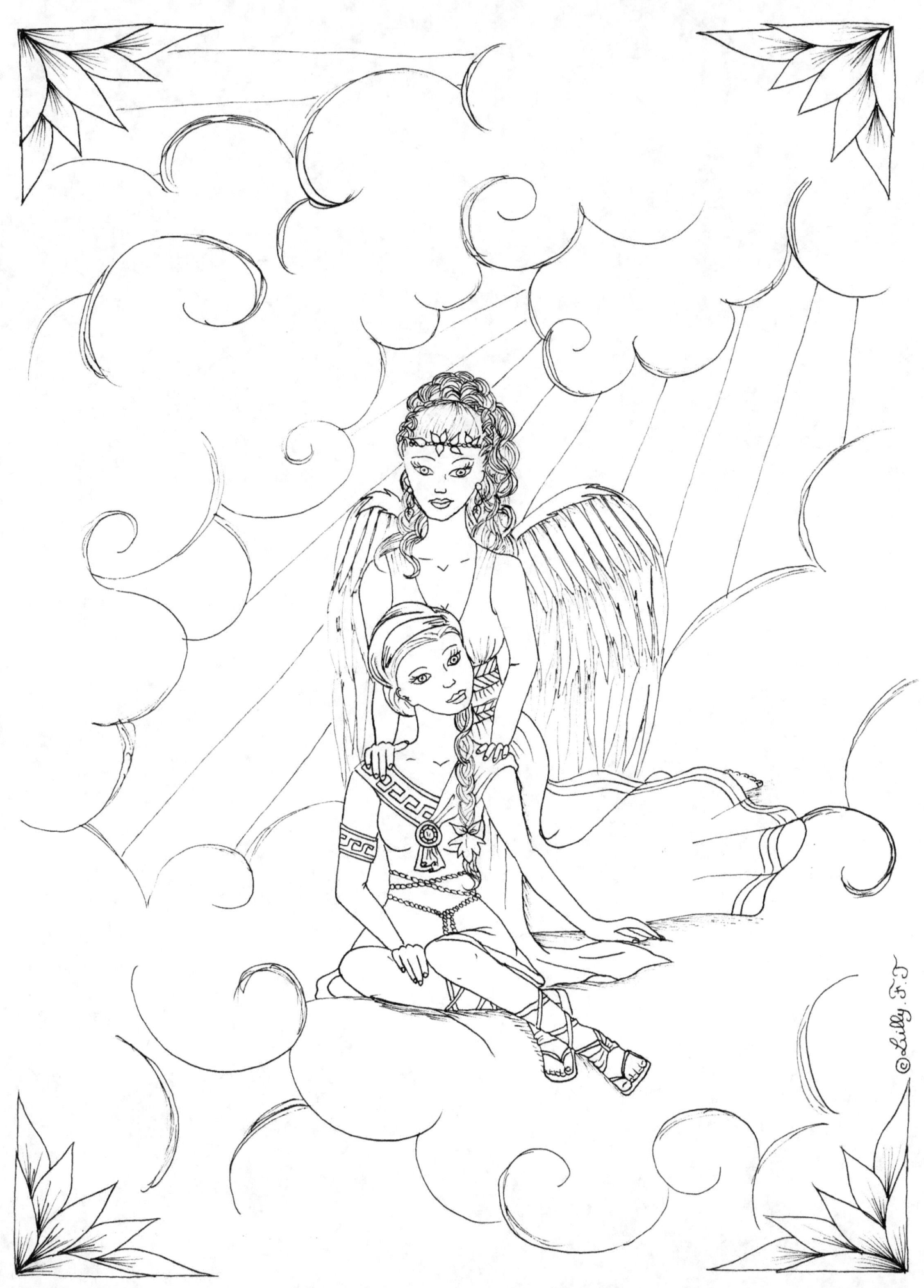

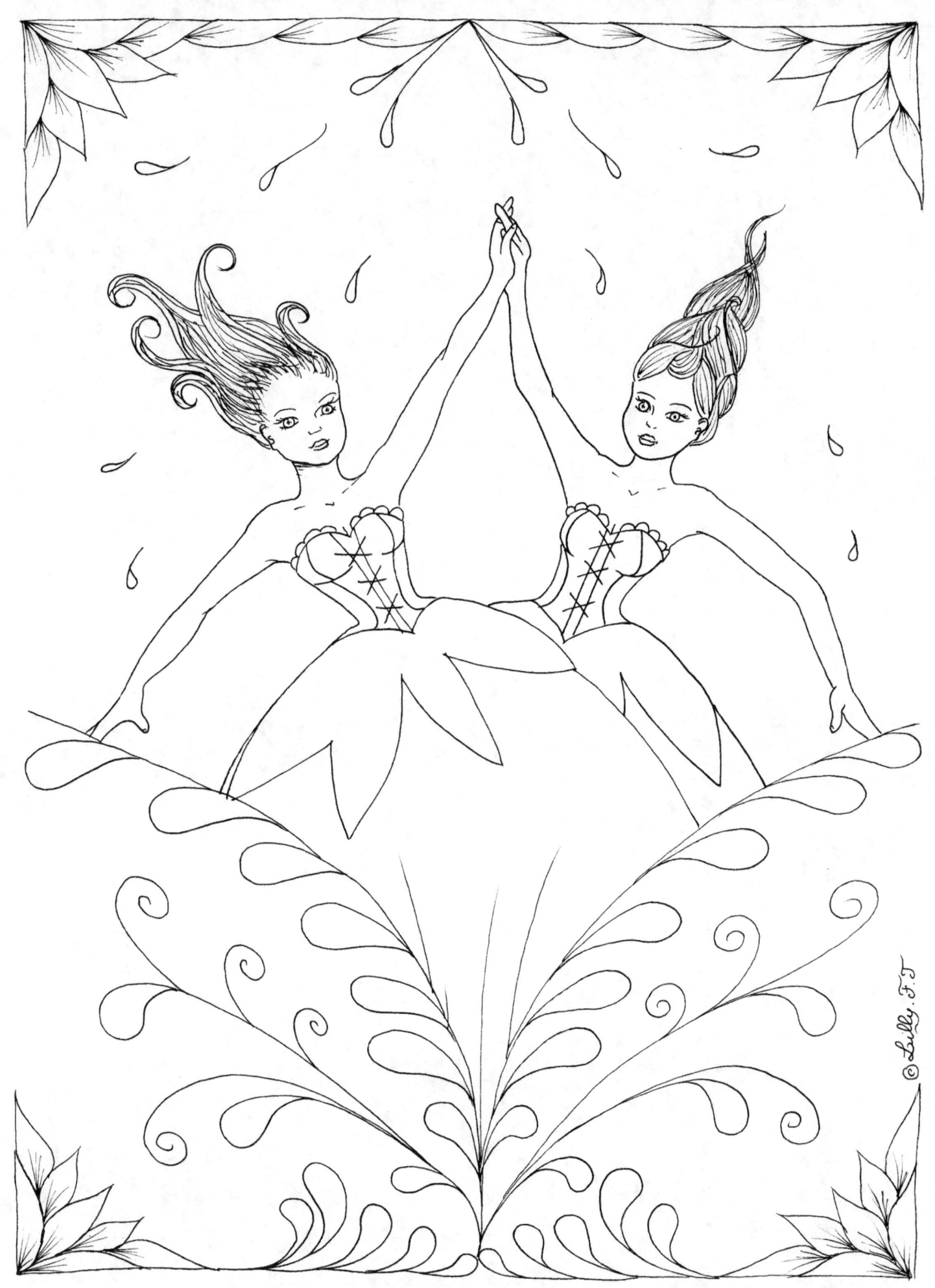

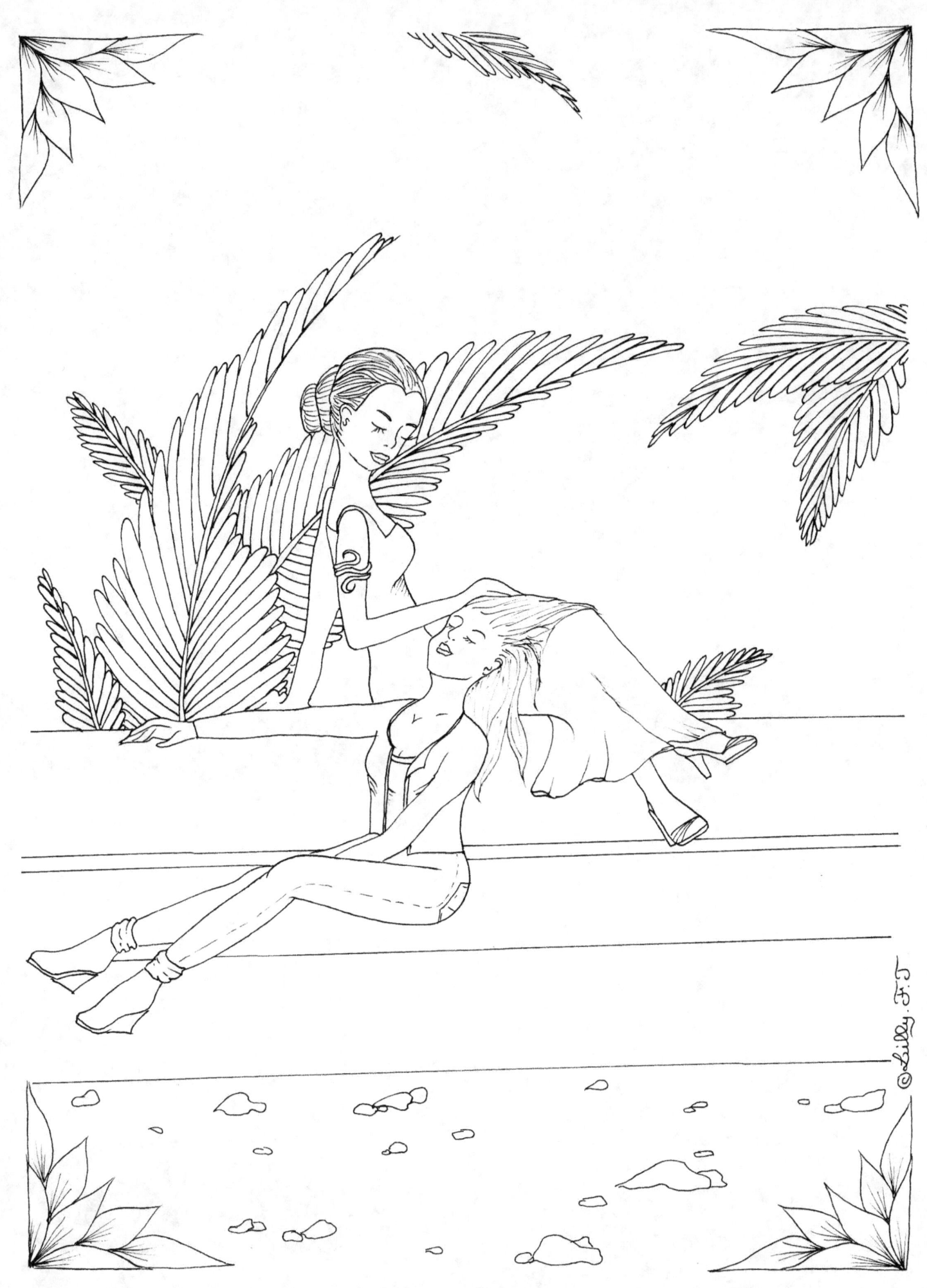

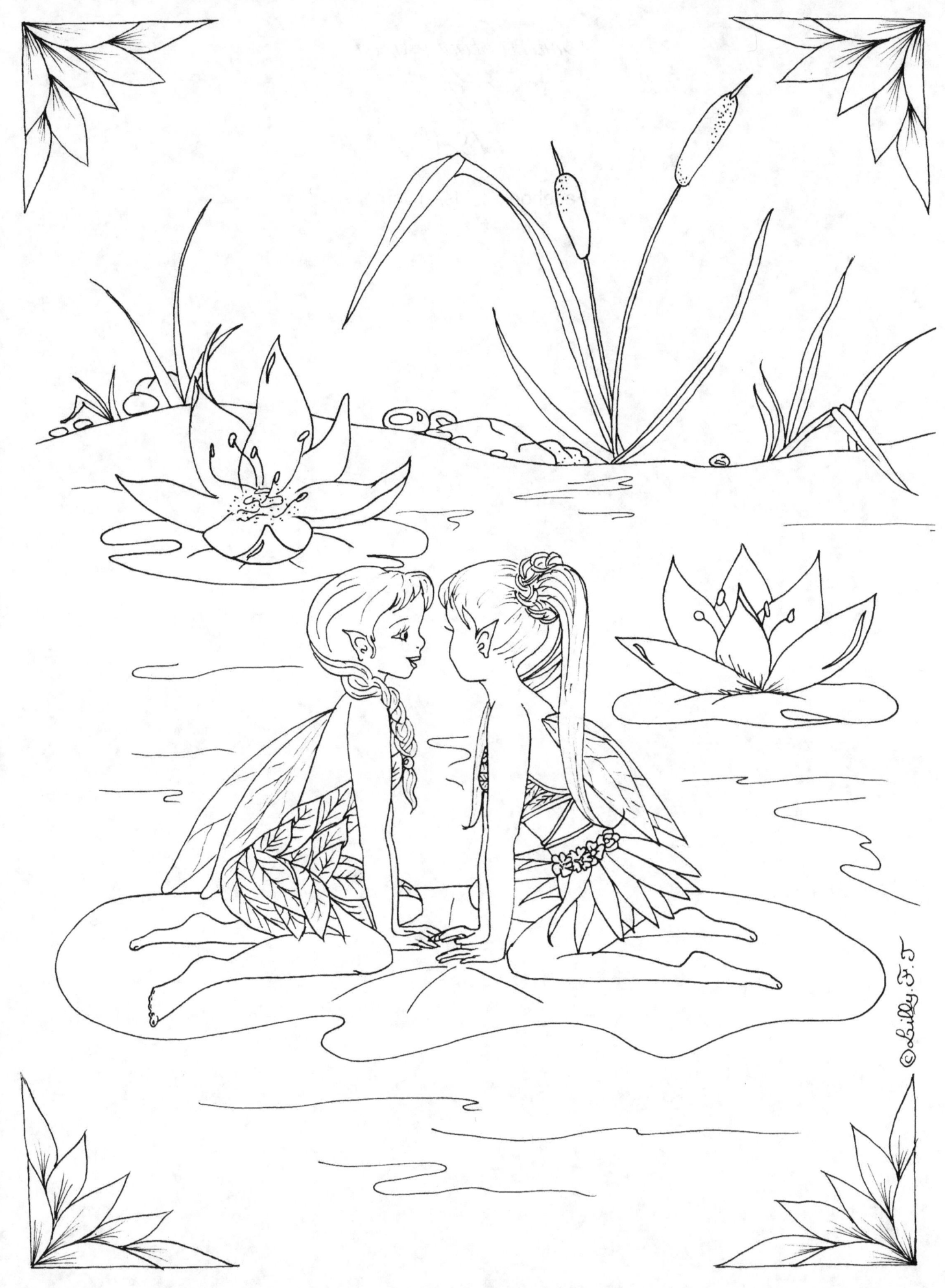

Contributing Artist
T.J.
USA

Facebook : TJsArtCorner

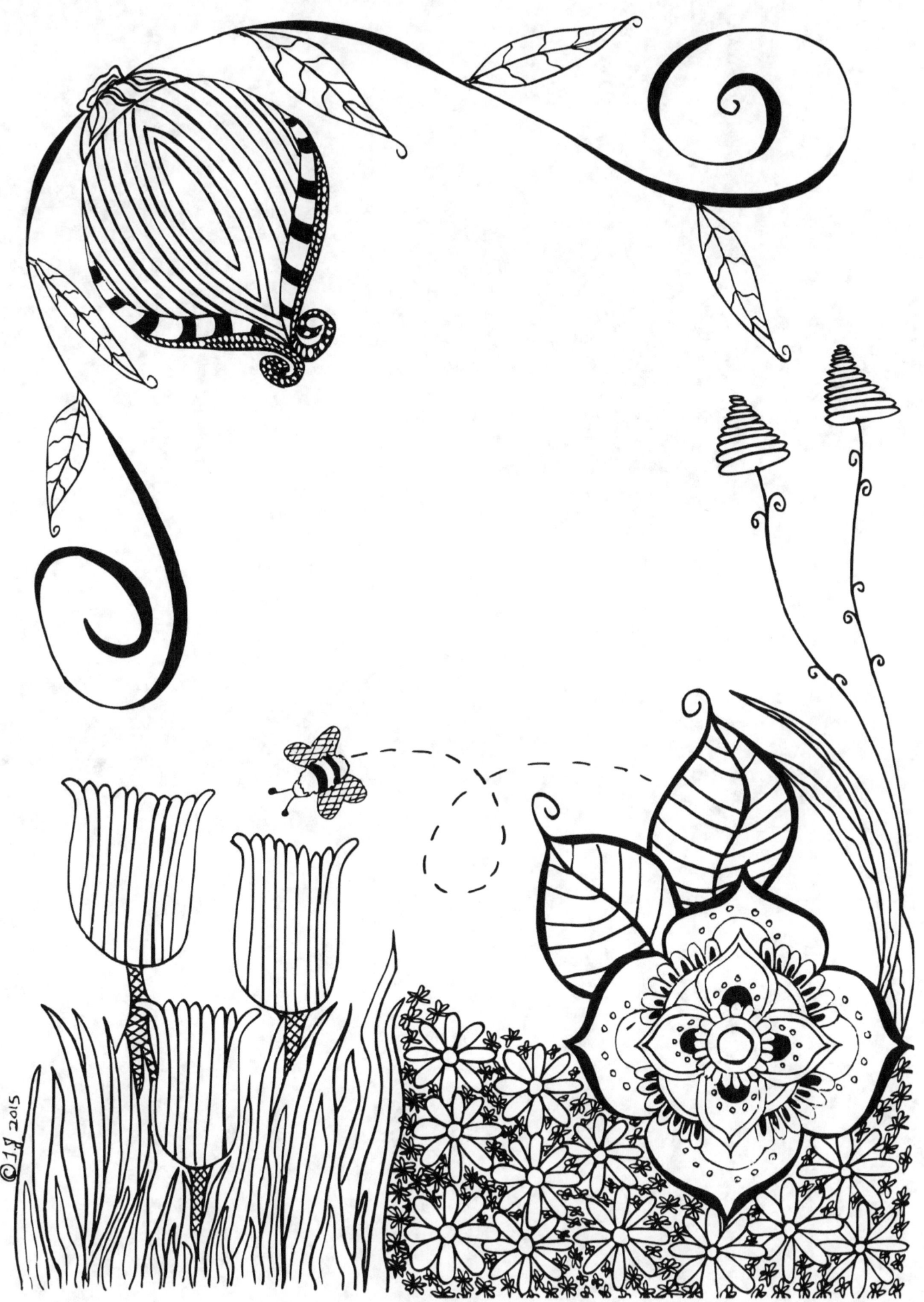

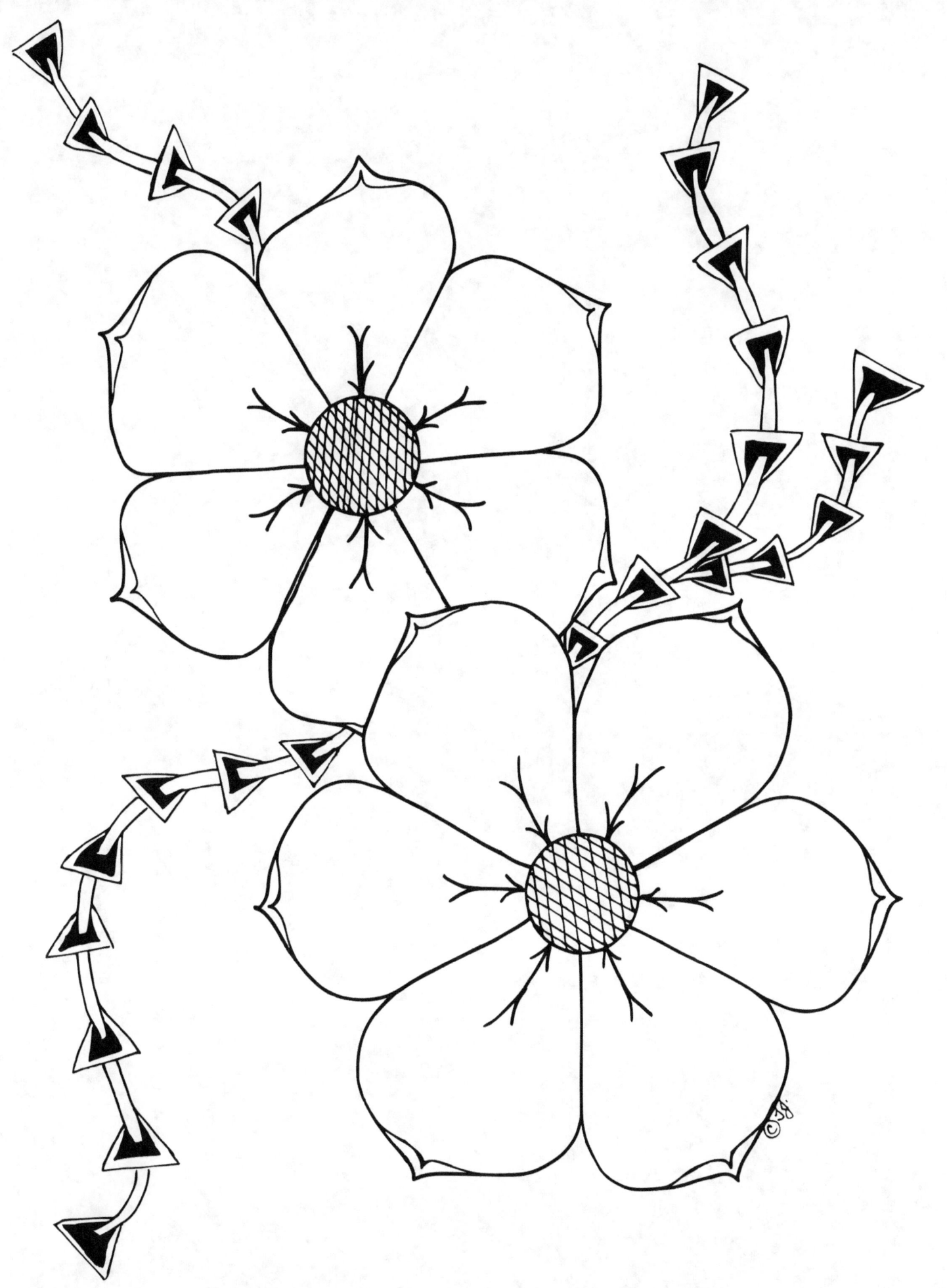

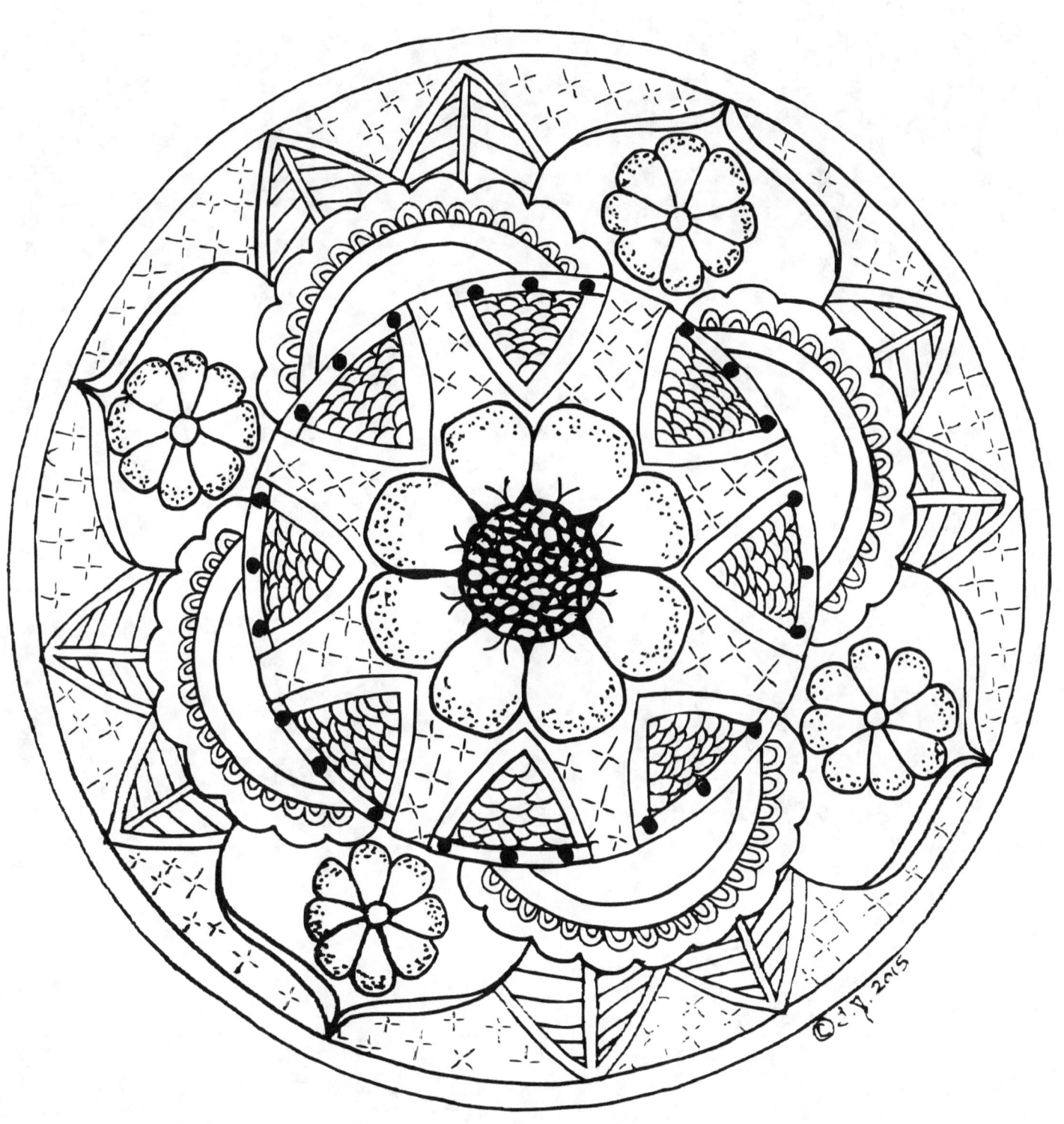

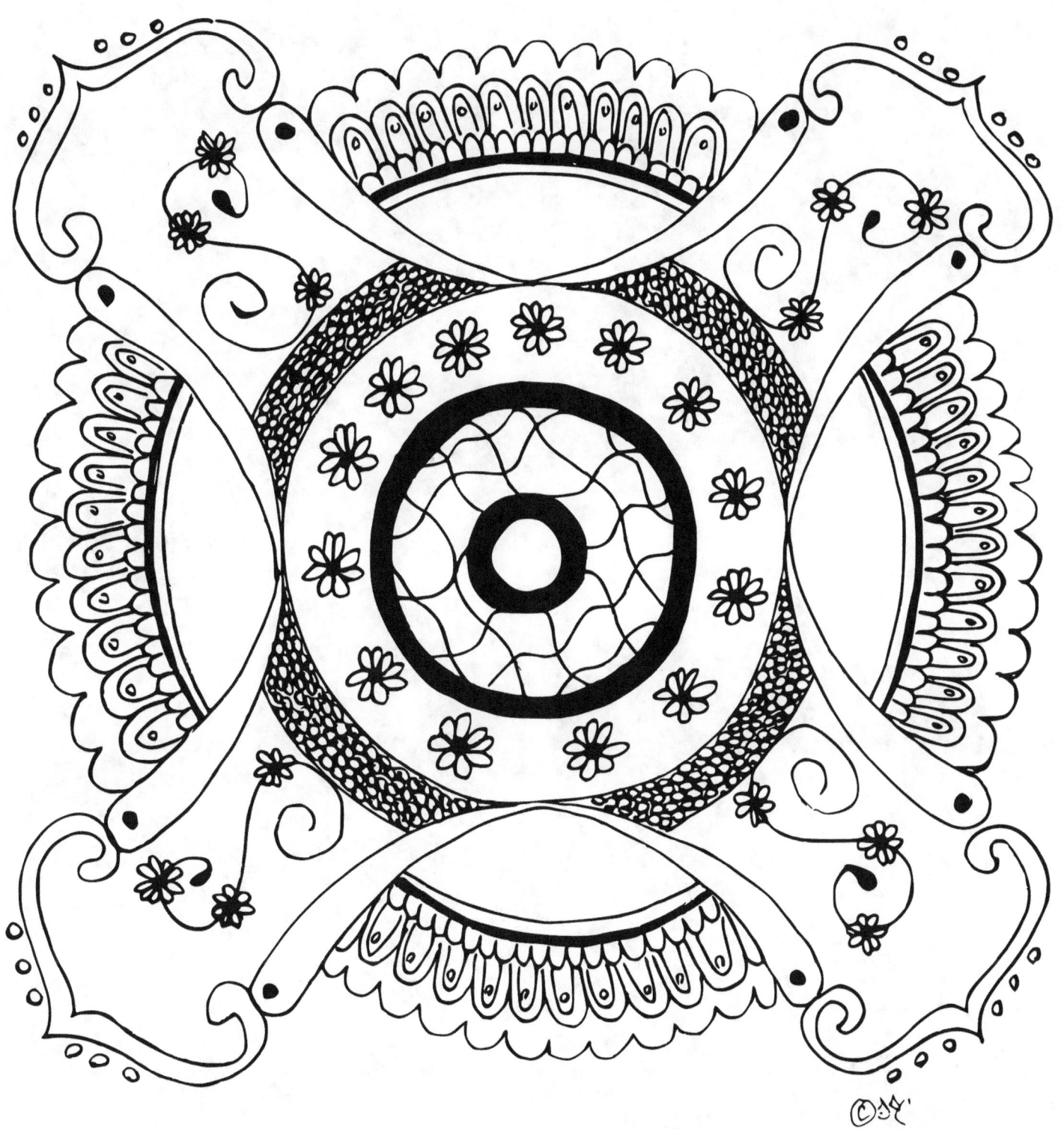

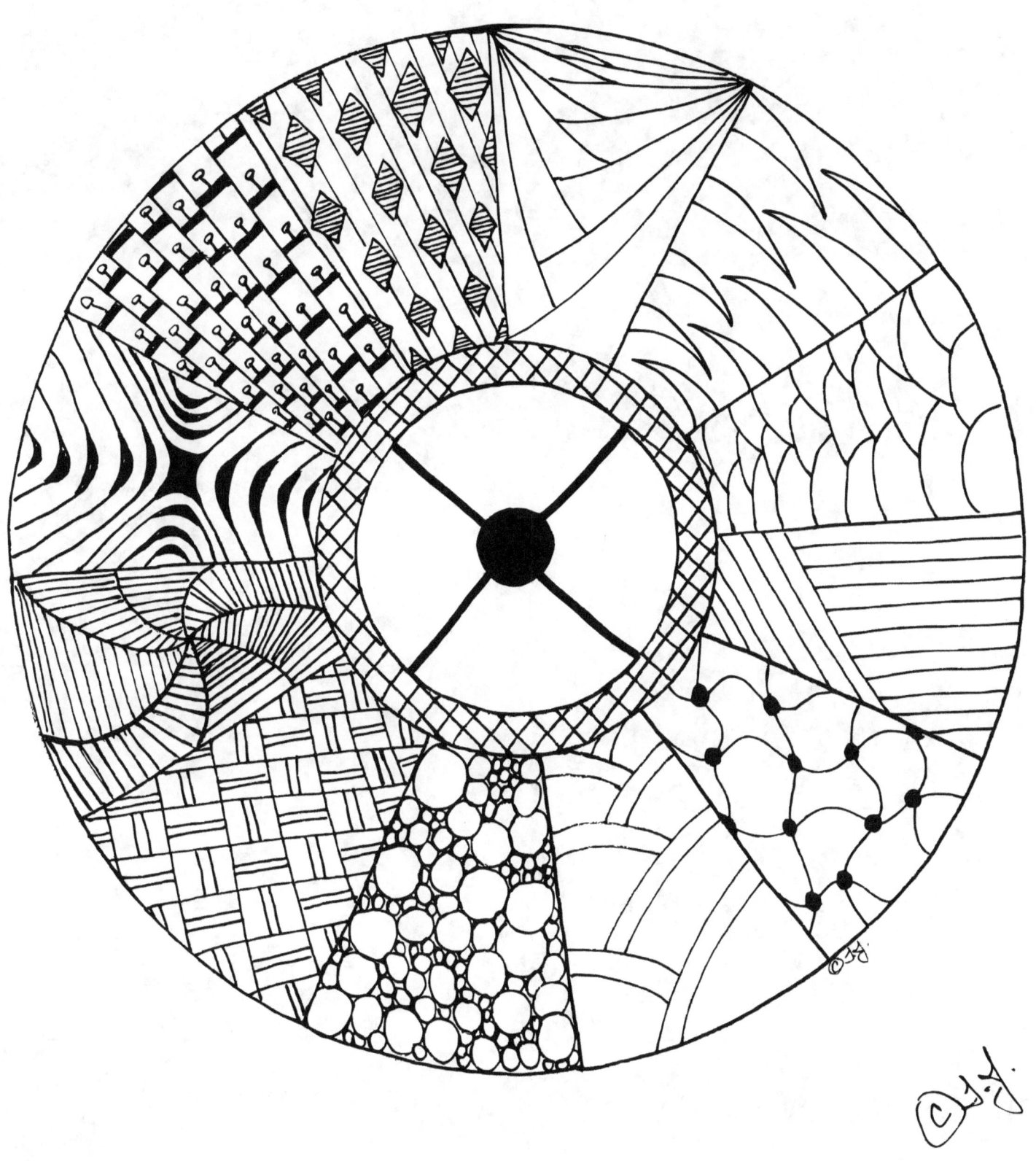

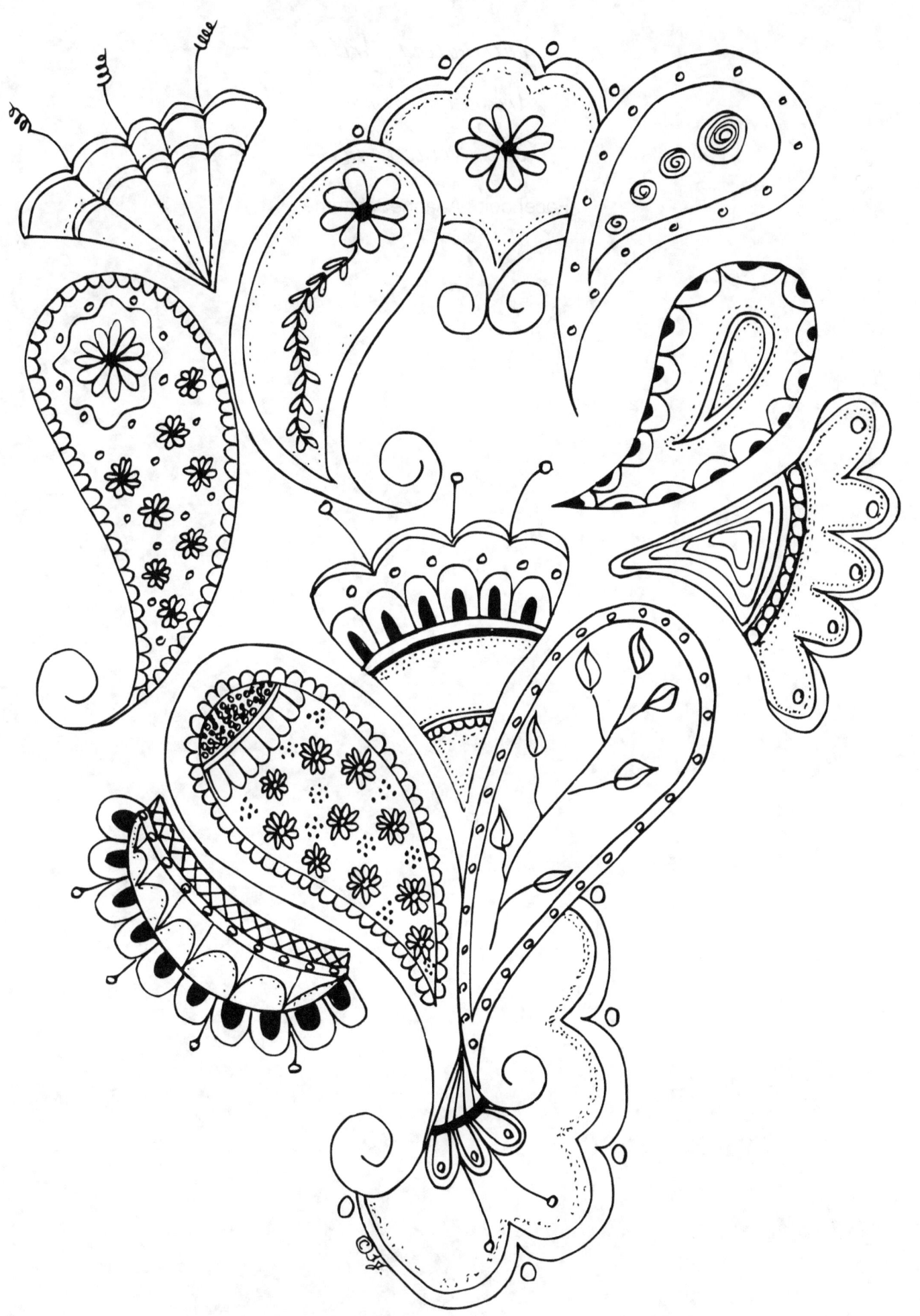

Contributing Artist
Arianne Schimmel
The Netherlands

Facebook : ArianneSchimmel

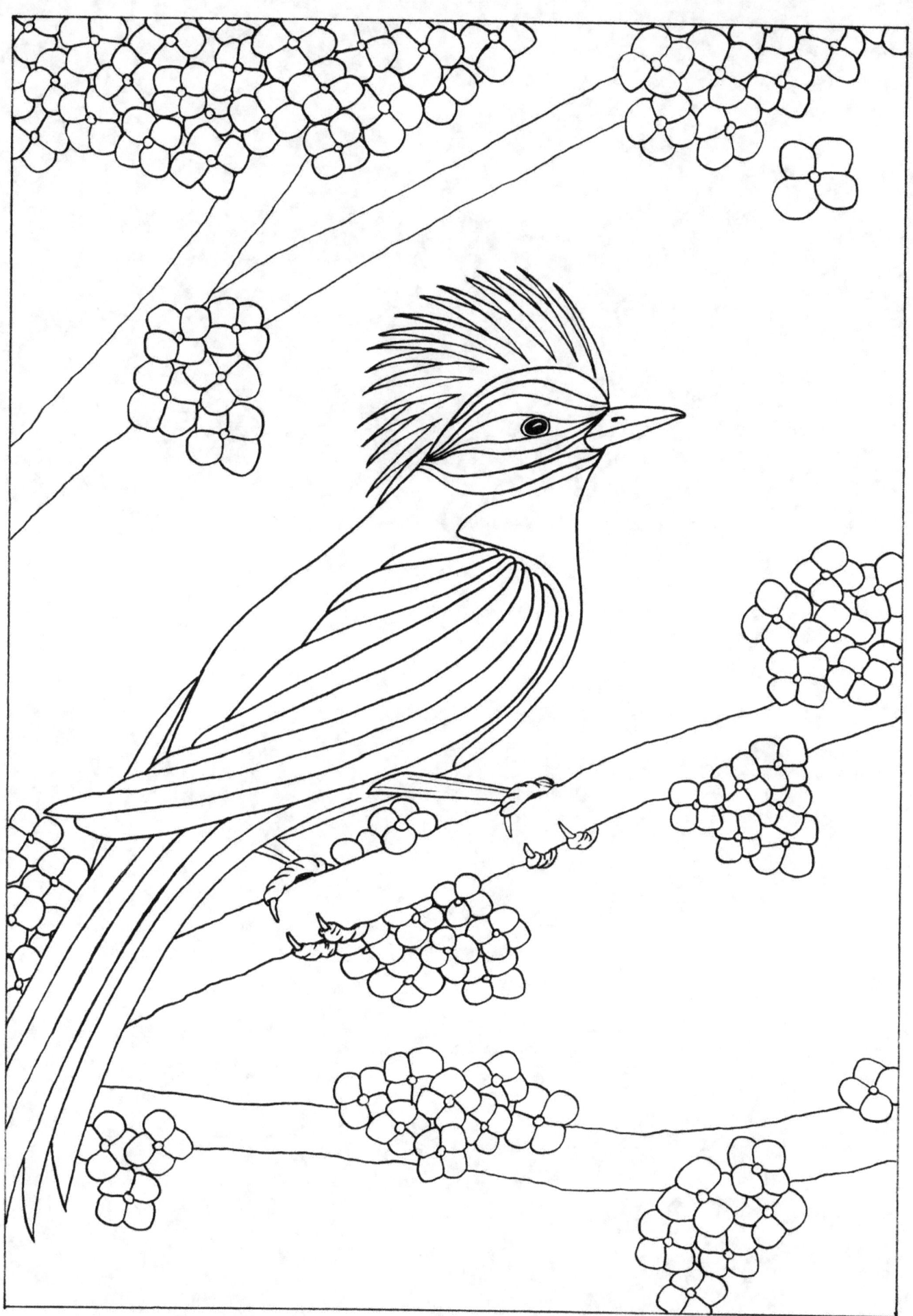

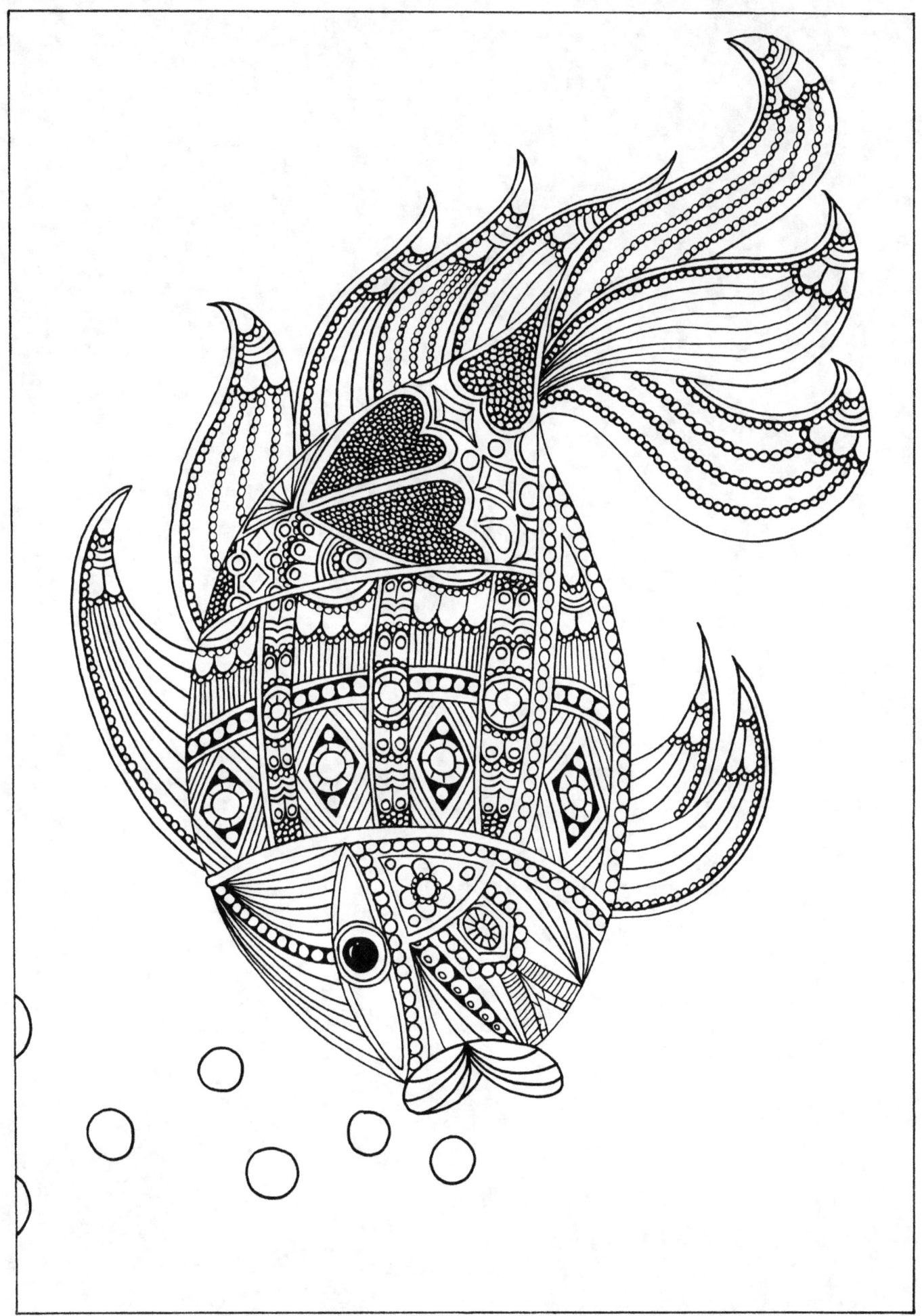

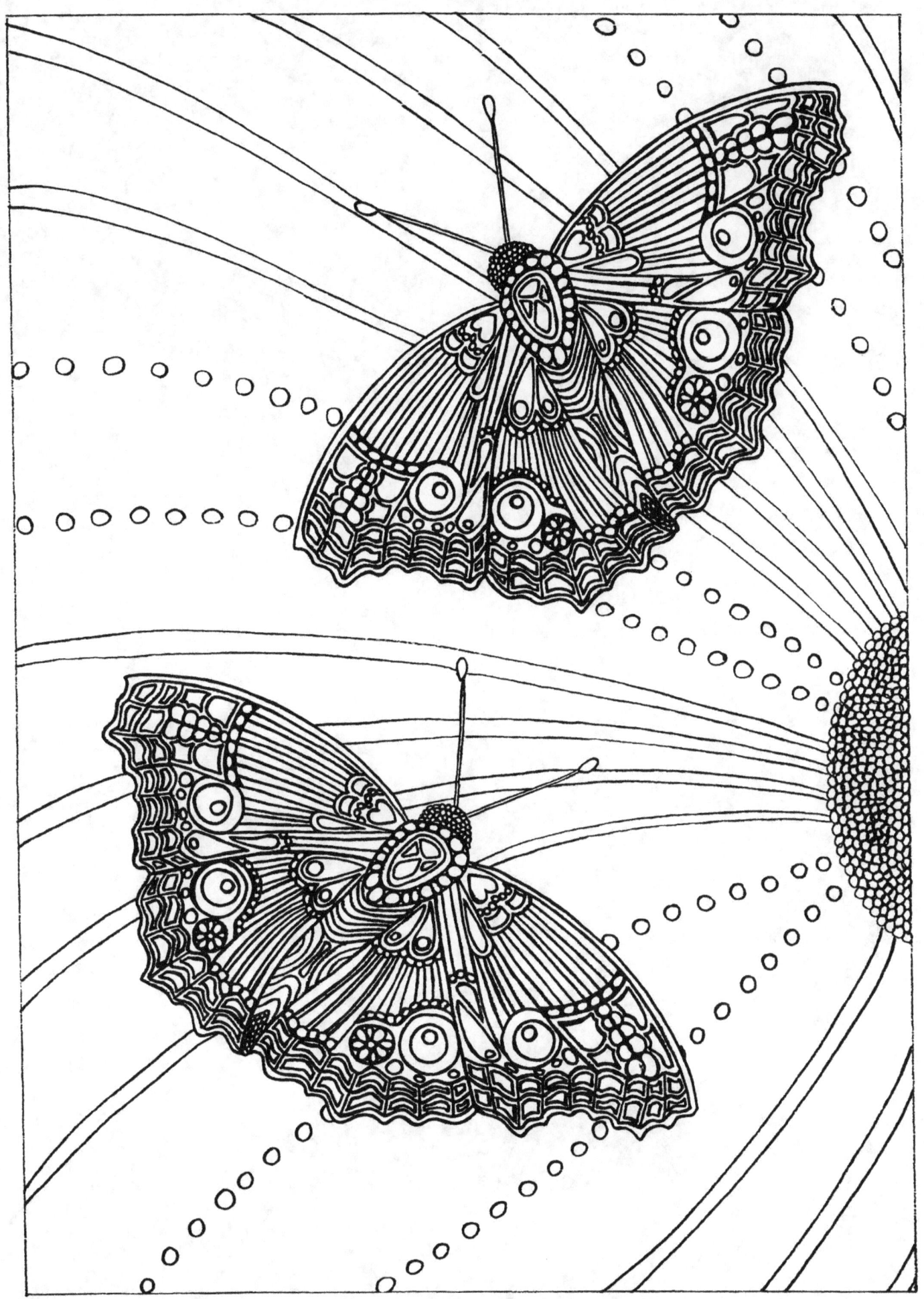

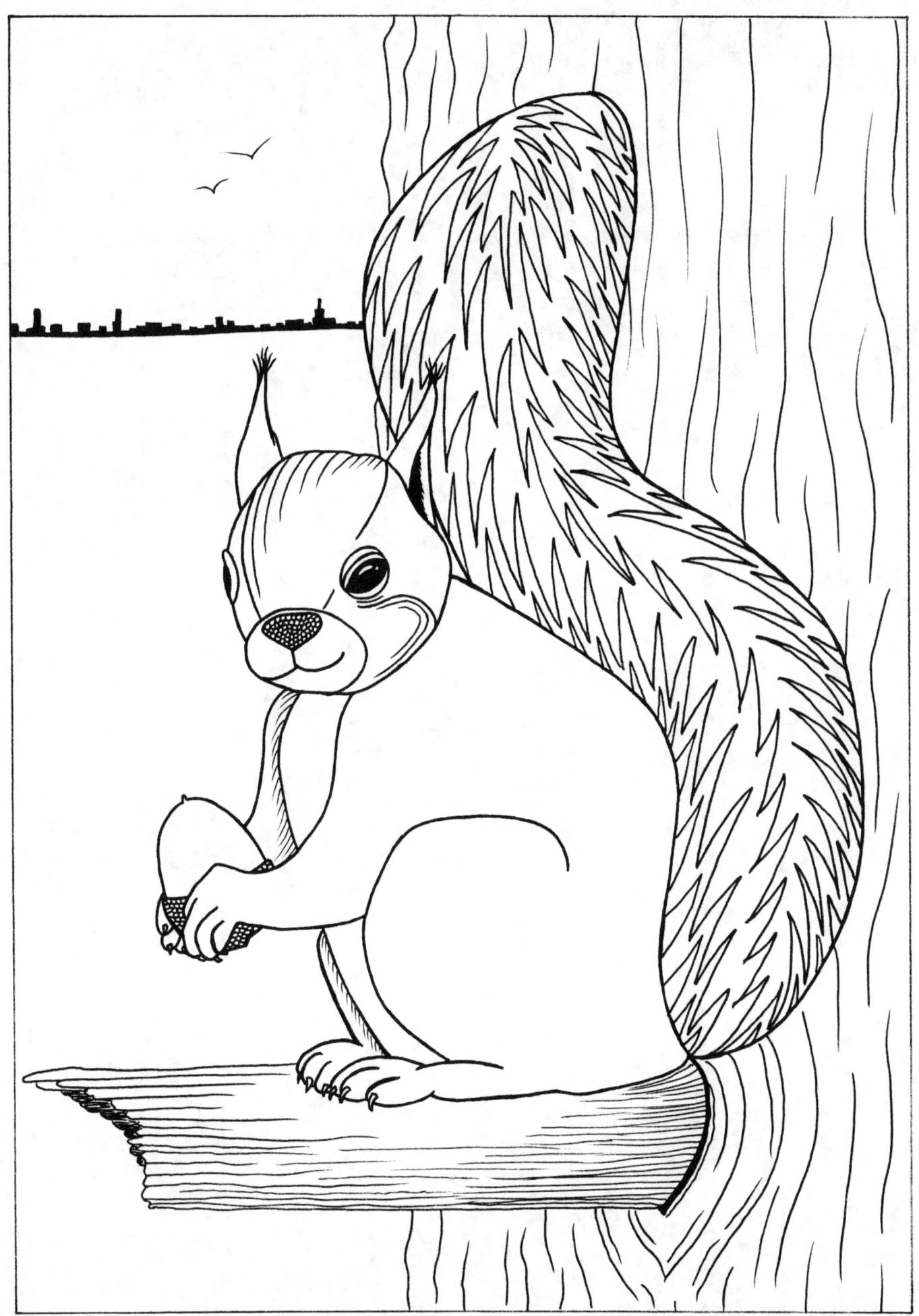

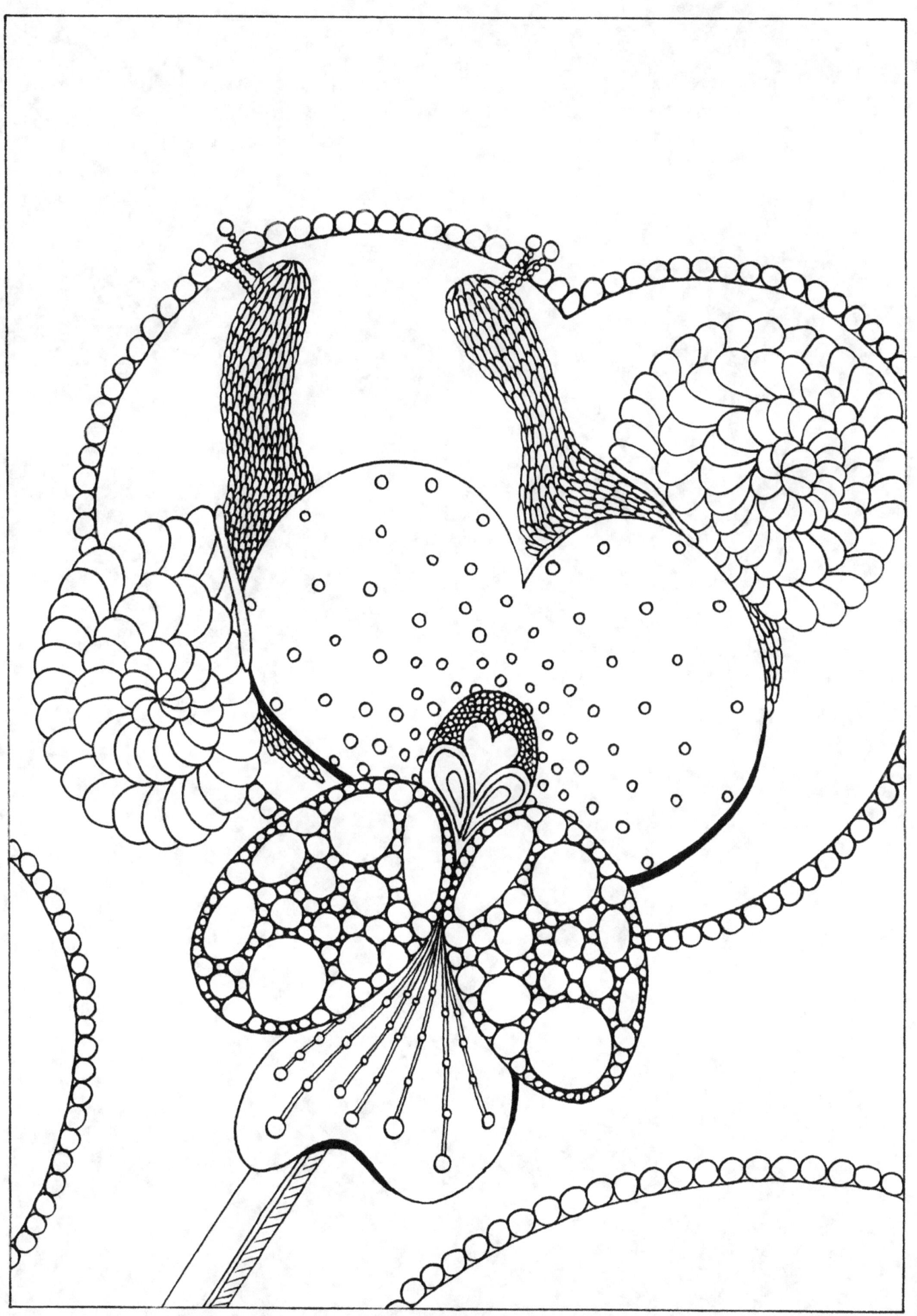

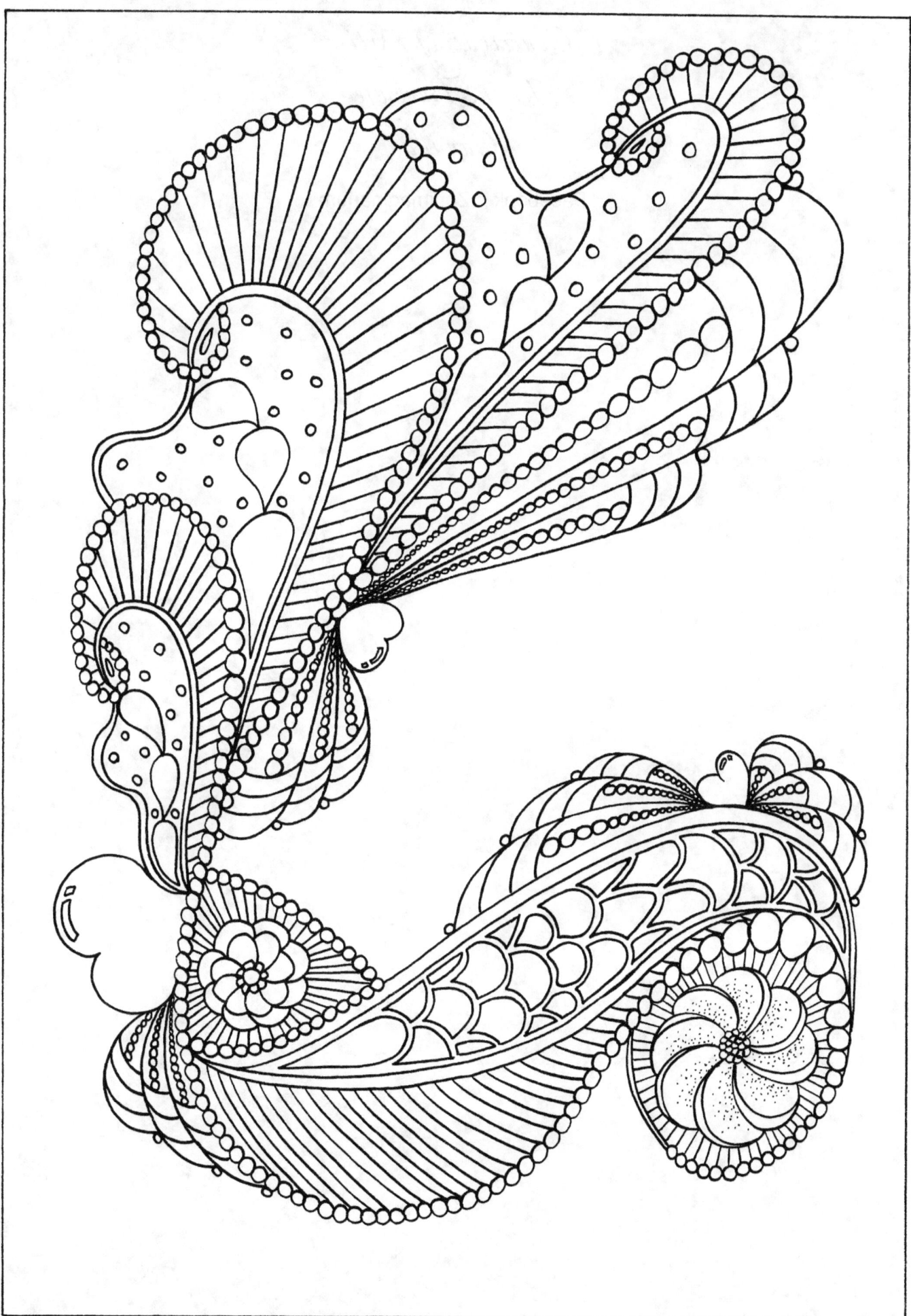

Contributing Artist
Jeanne Burbage
Canada

Facebook : Zenimaginarium

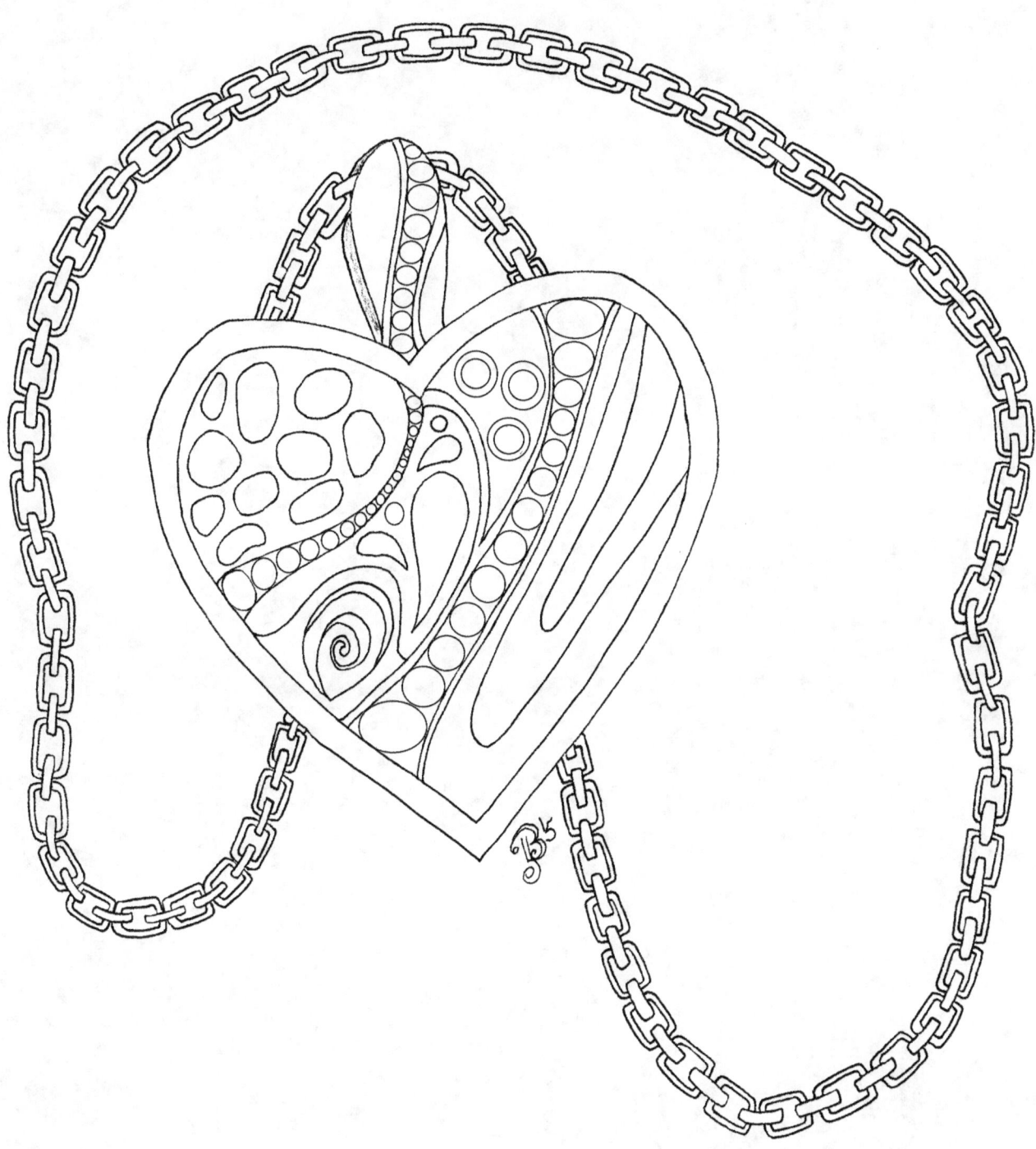

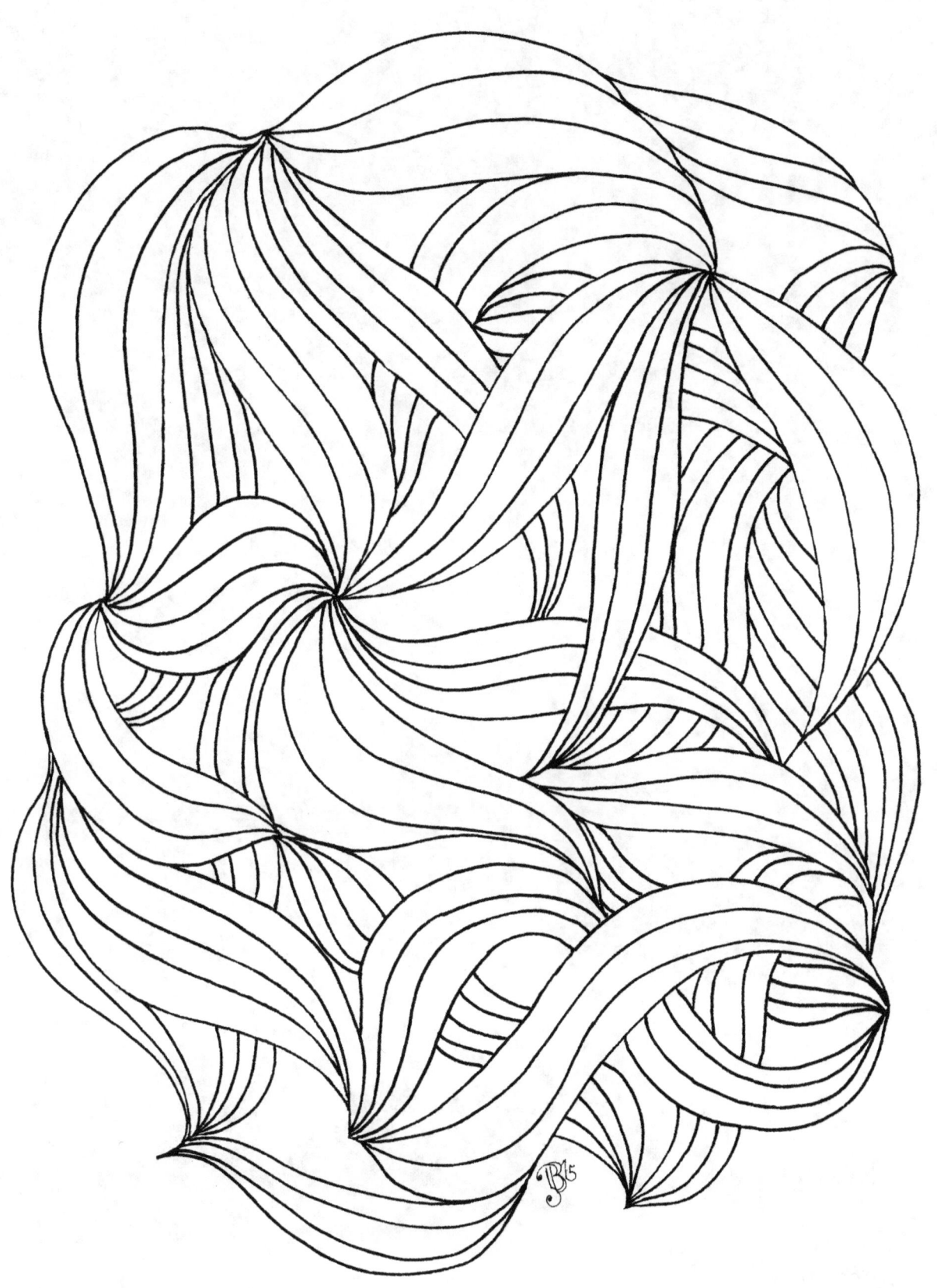

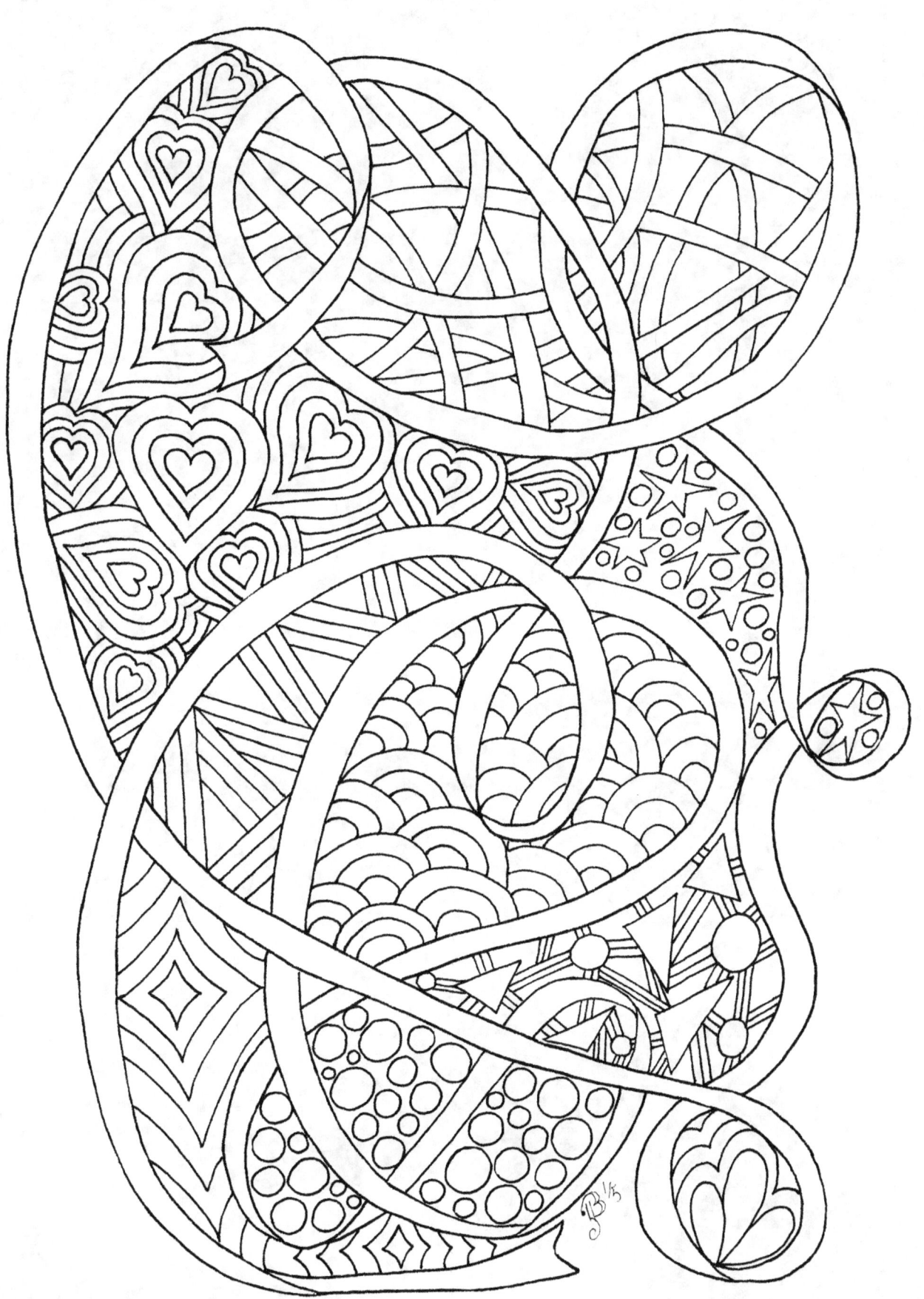

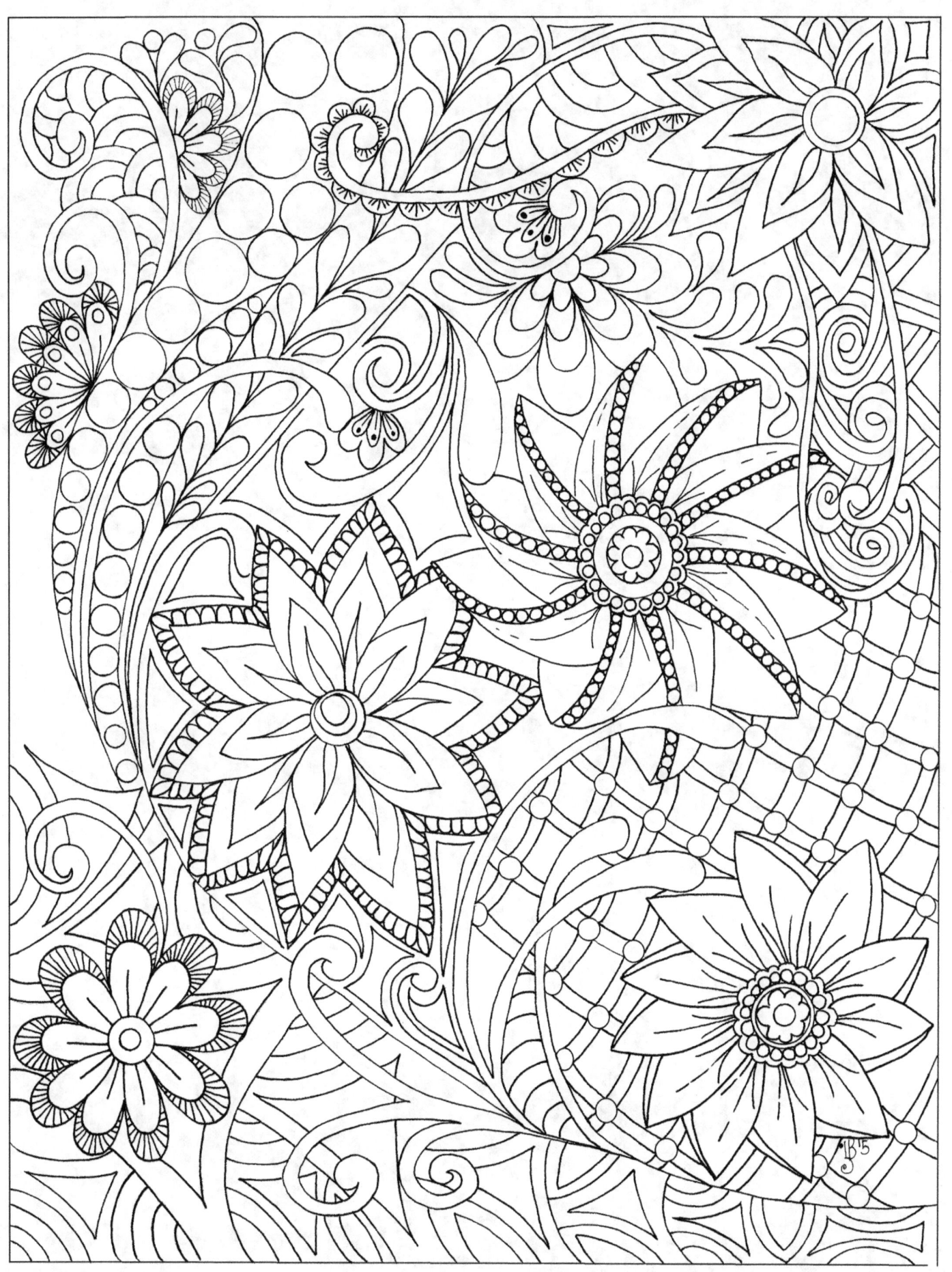

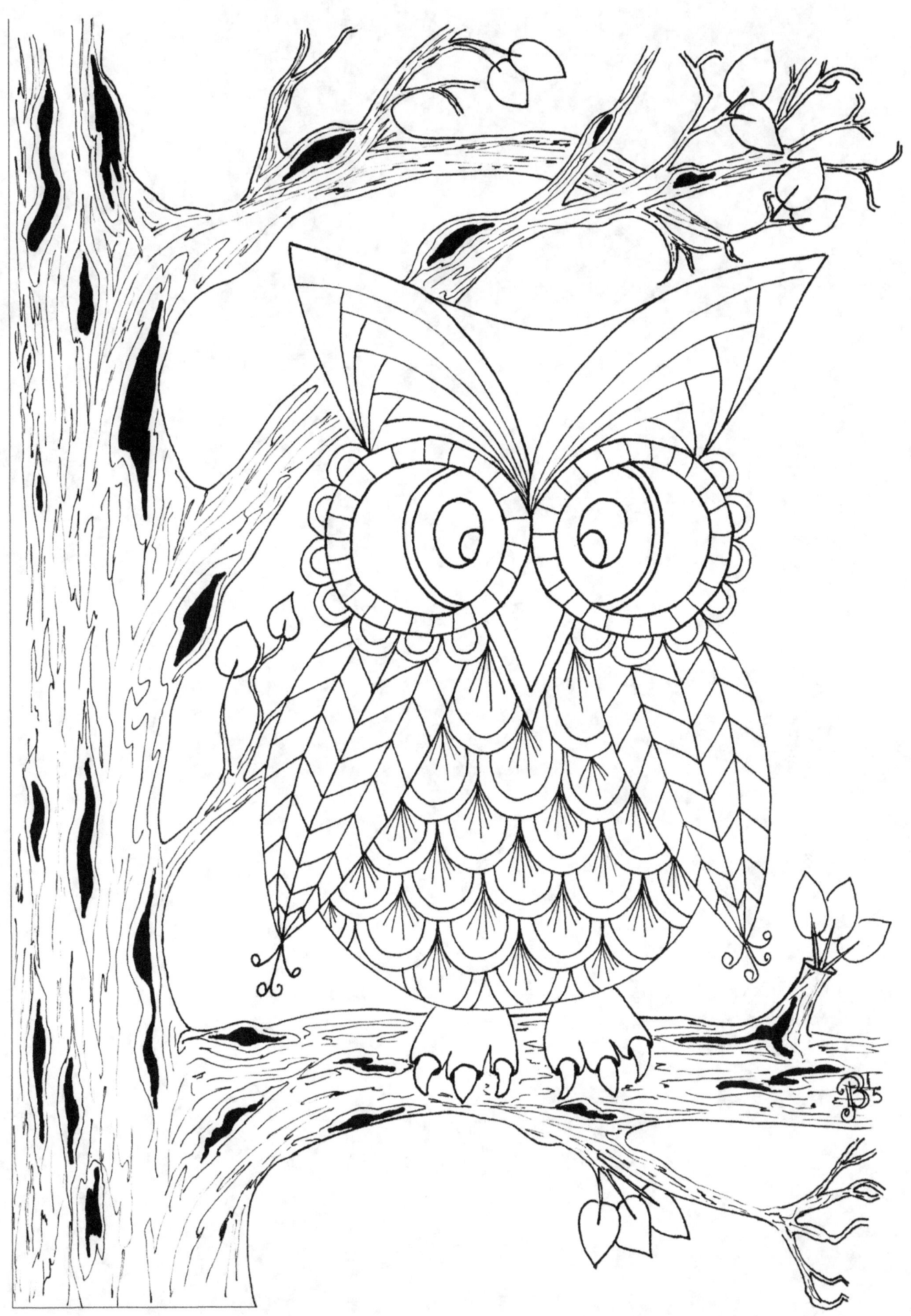

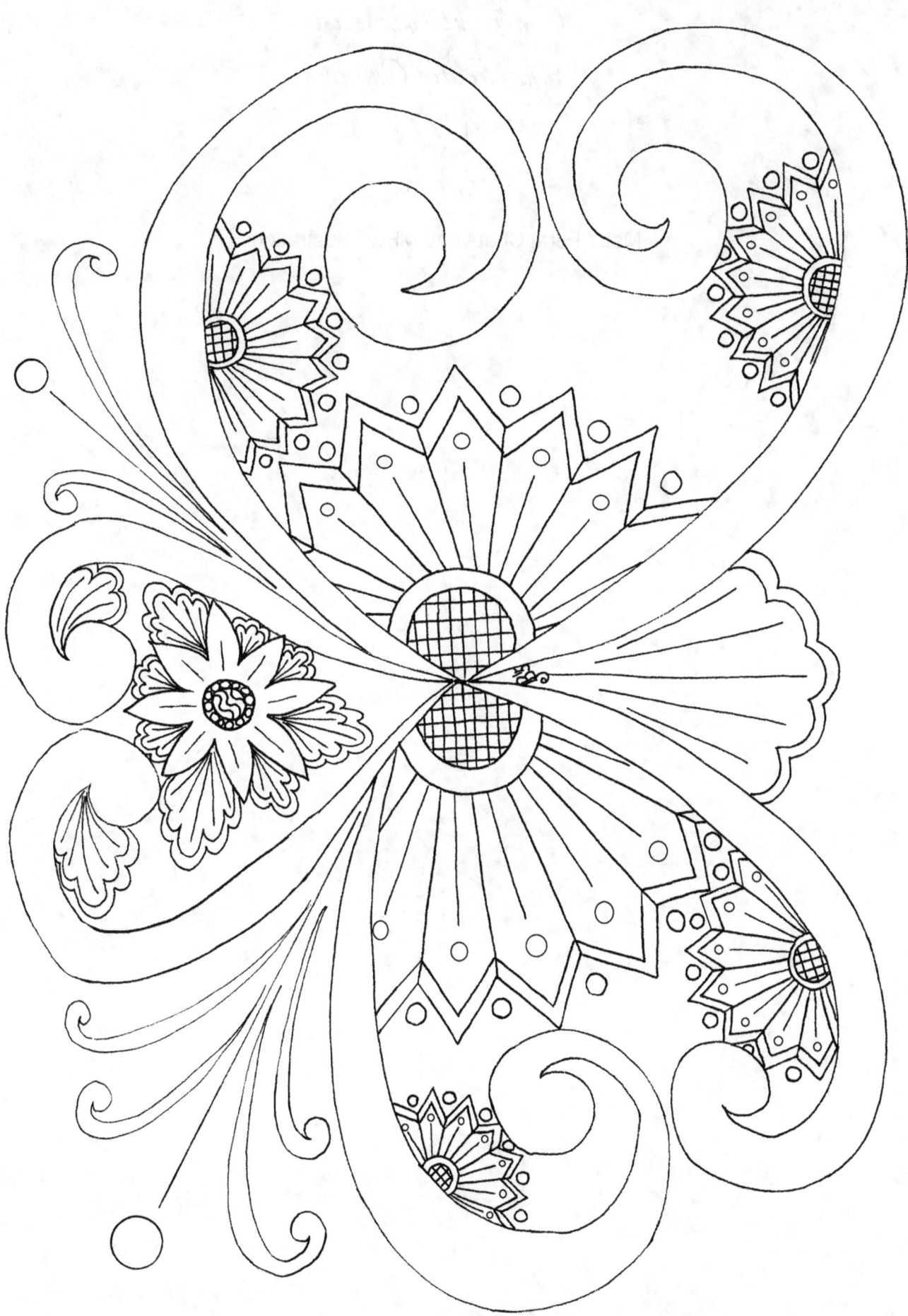

Contributing Artist
Maud Feral-Chauveau
MFC
France

Maud Feral Chauveau MFC - illustrations

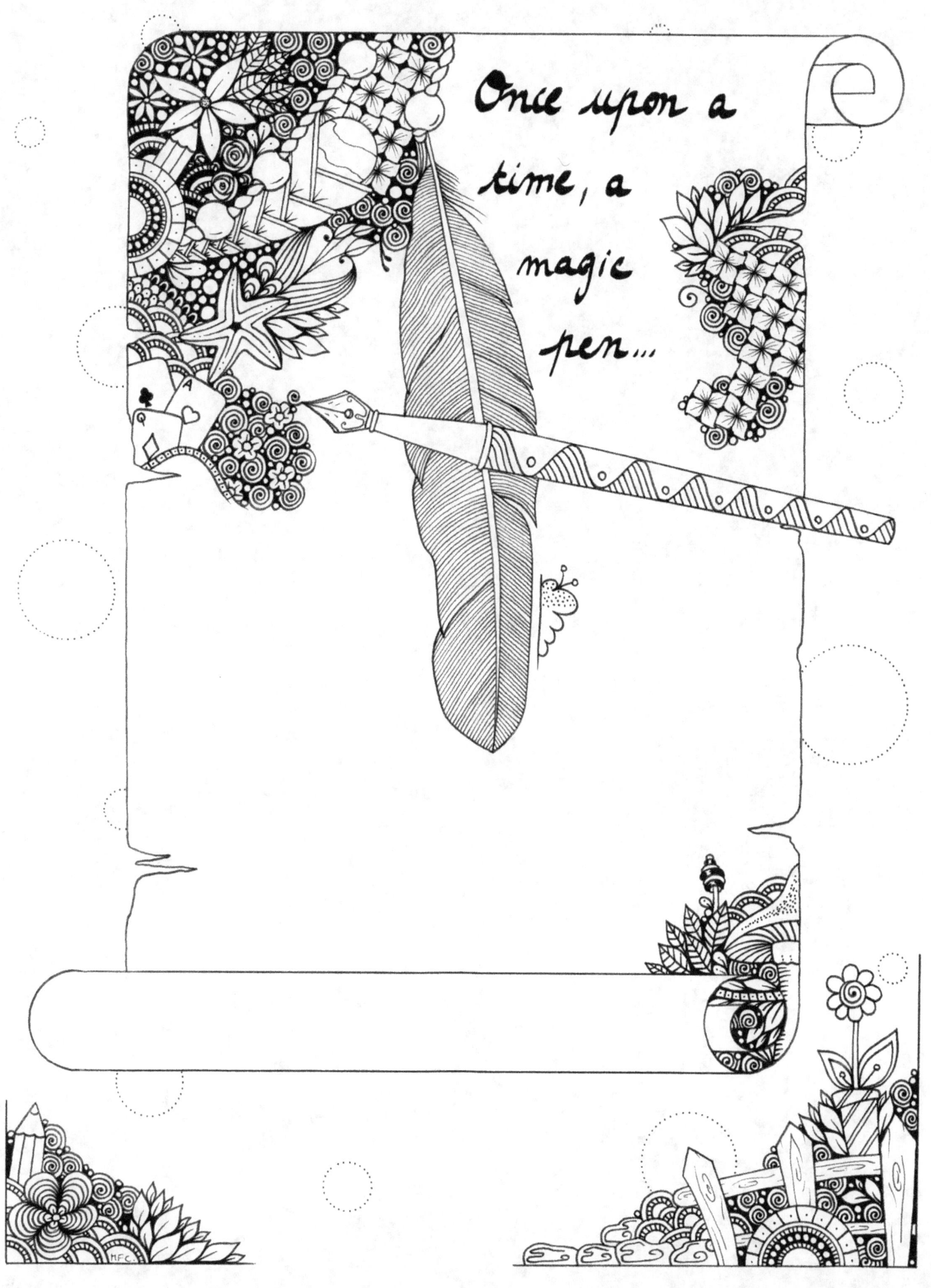

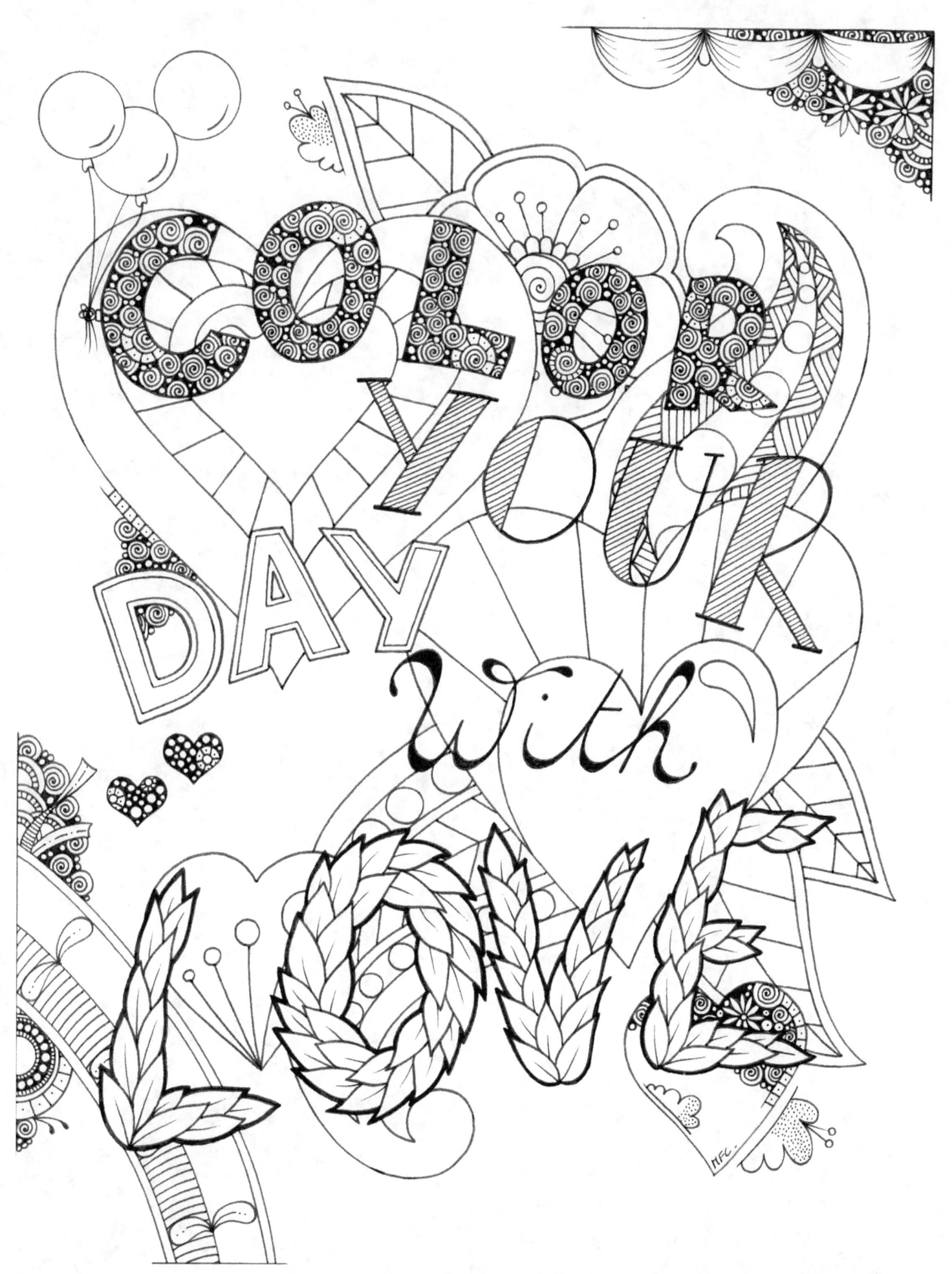

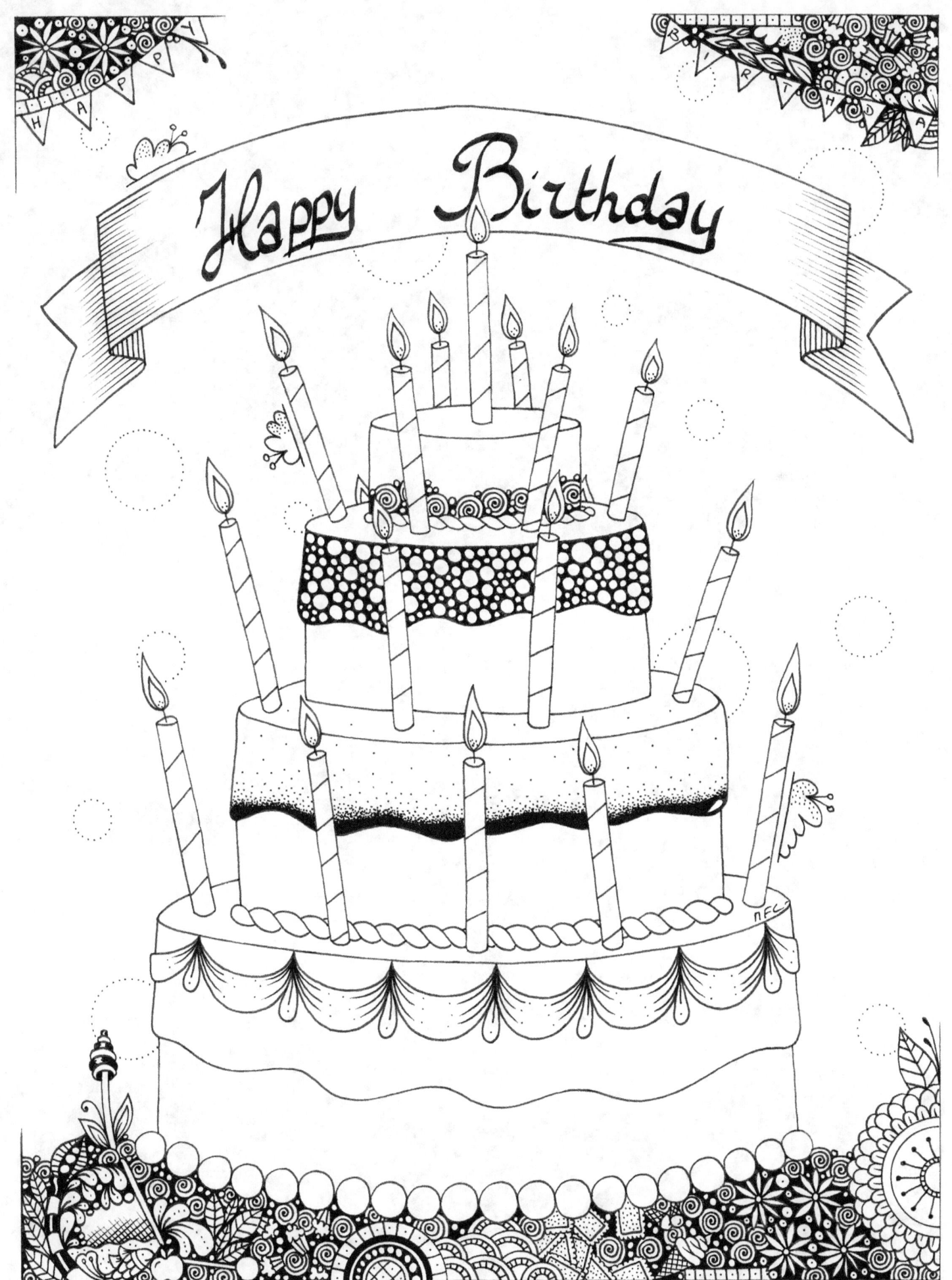

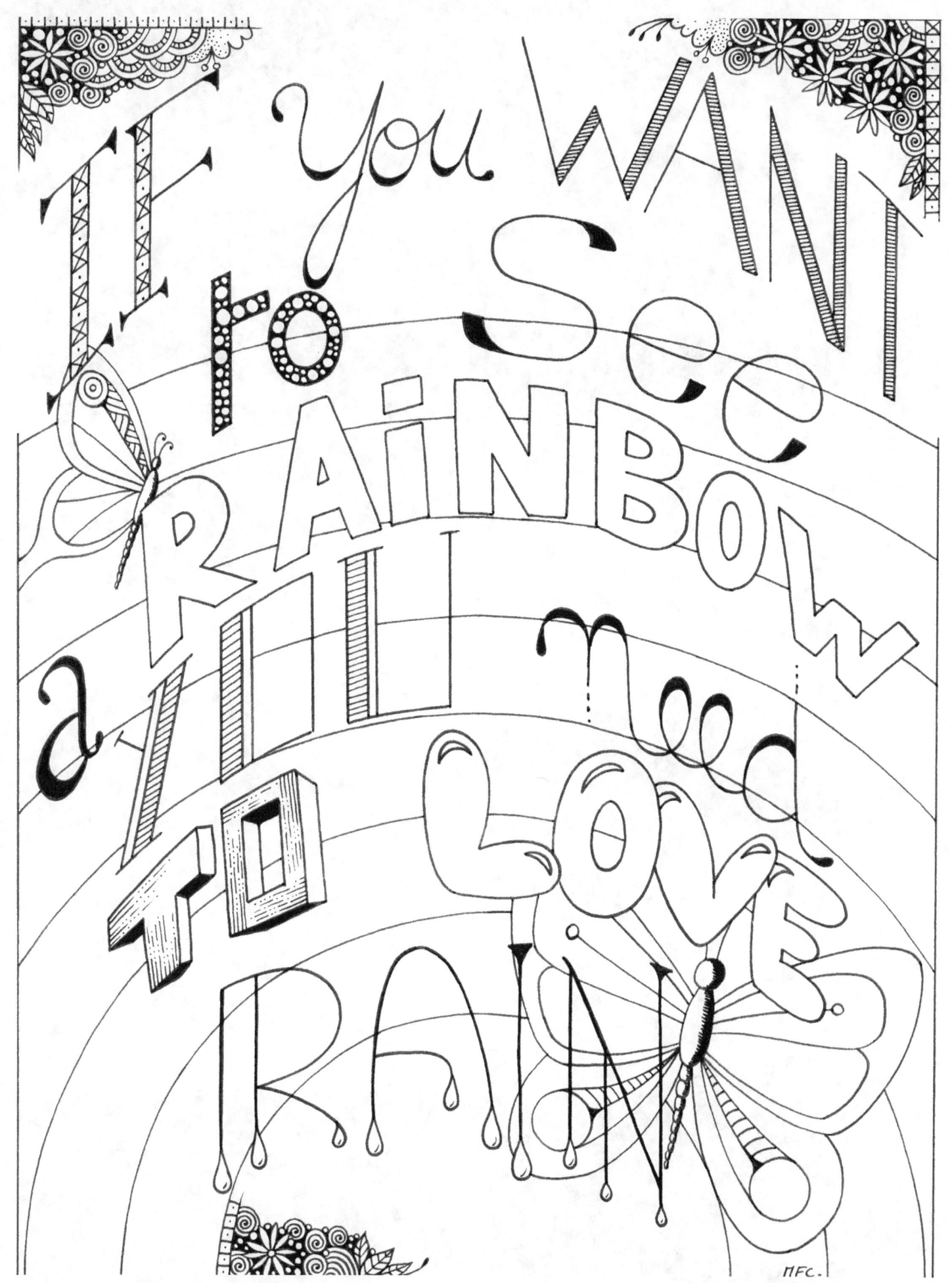

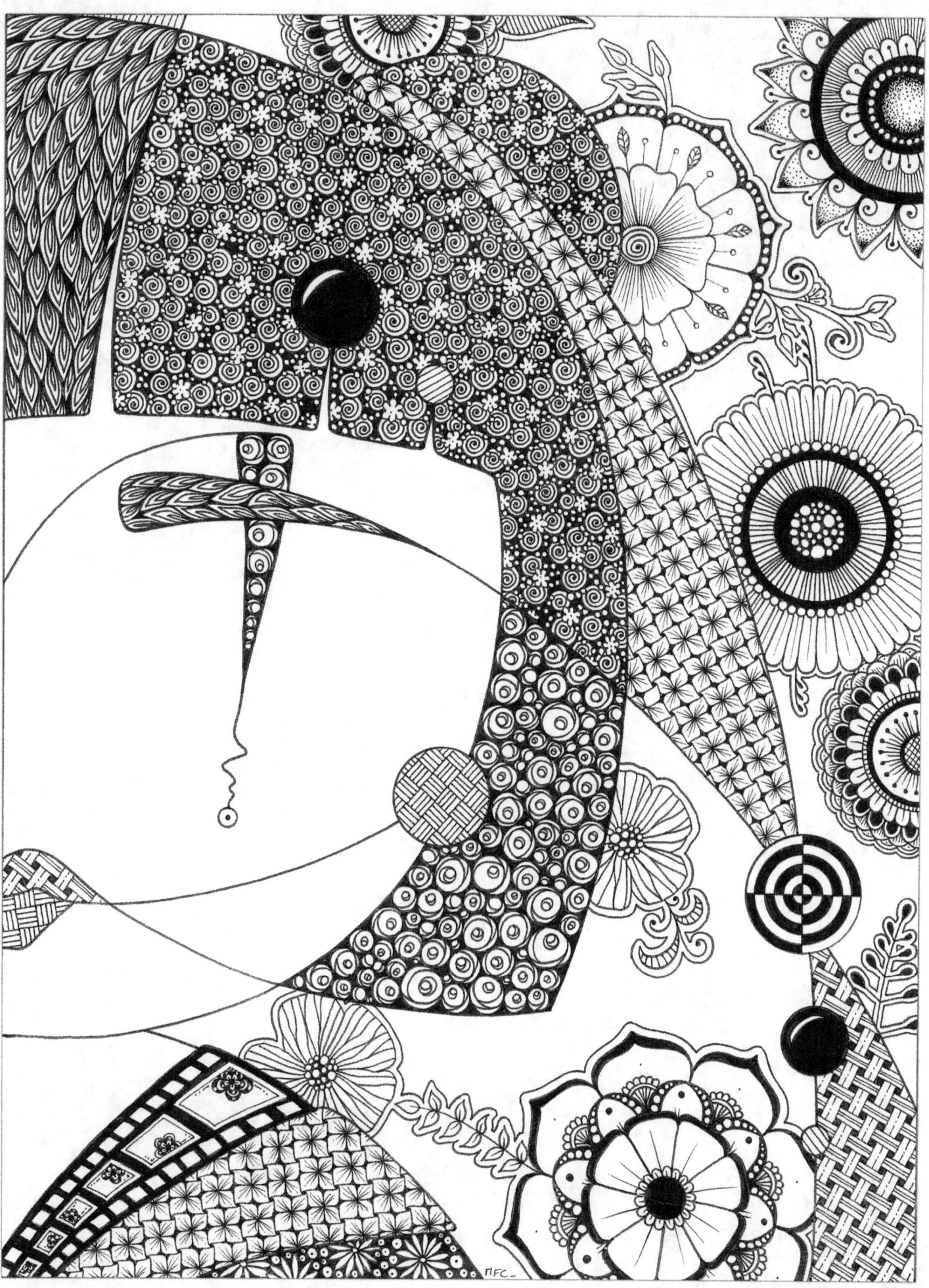

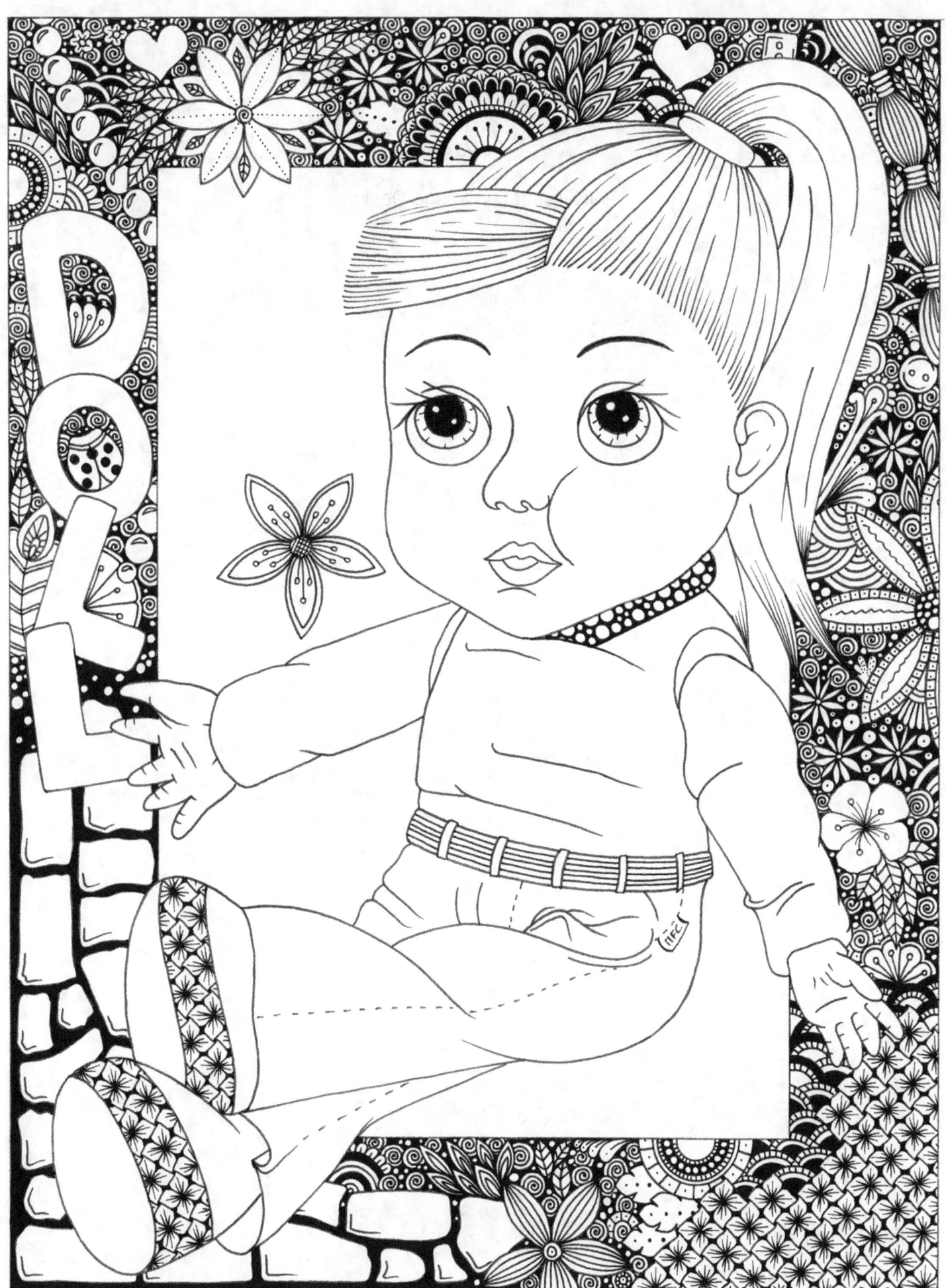

Contributing Artist
Jovian Ke
Taiwan

JK Illustration Image Design

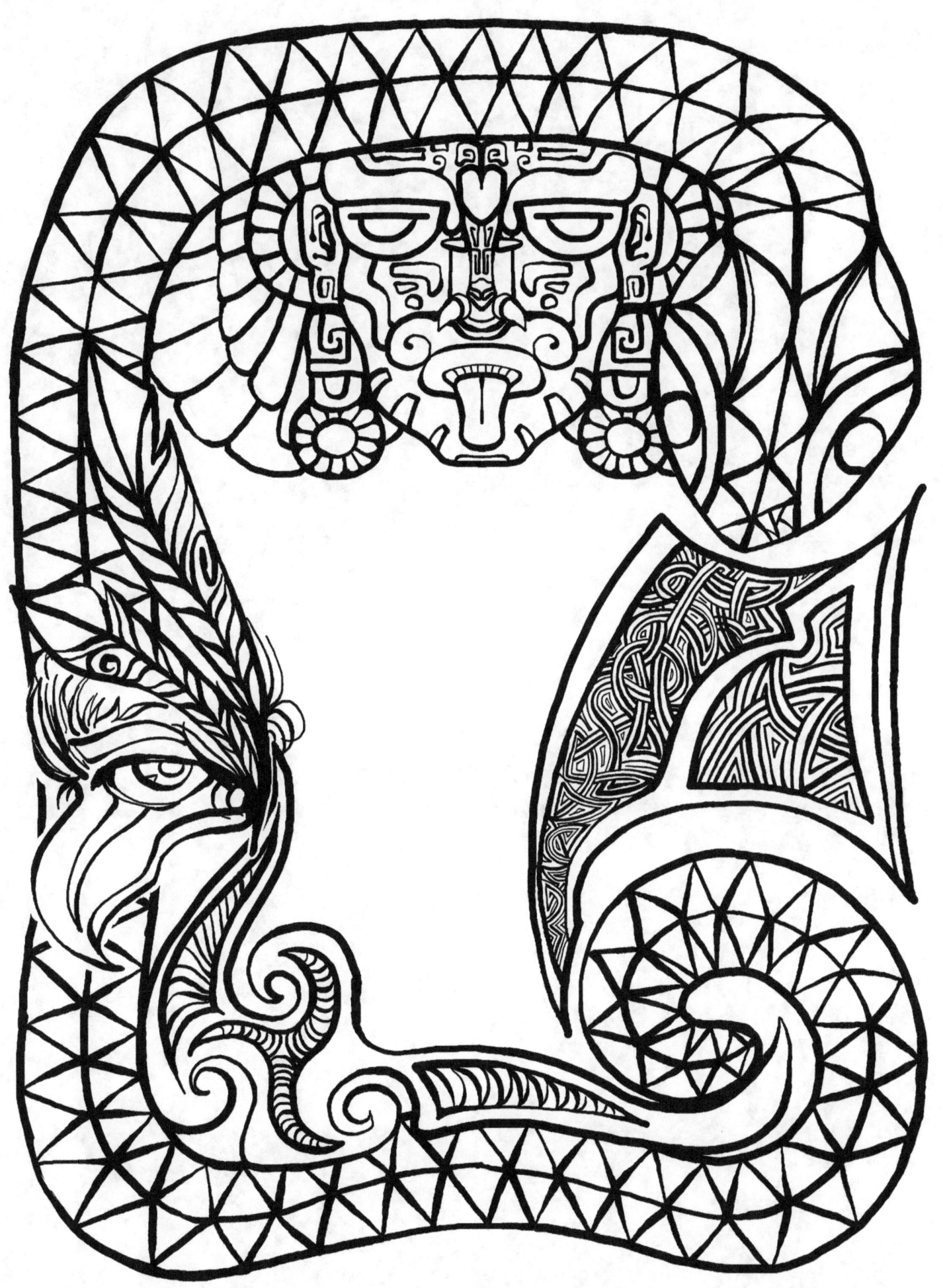

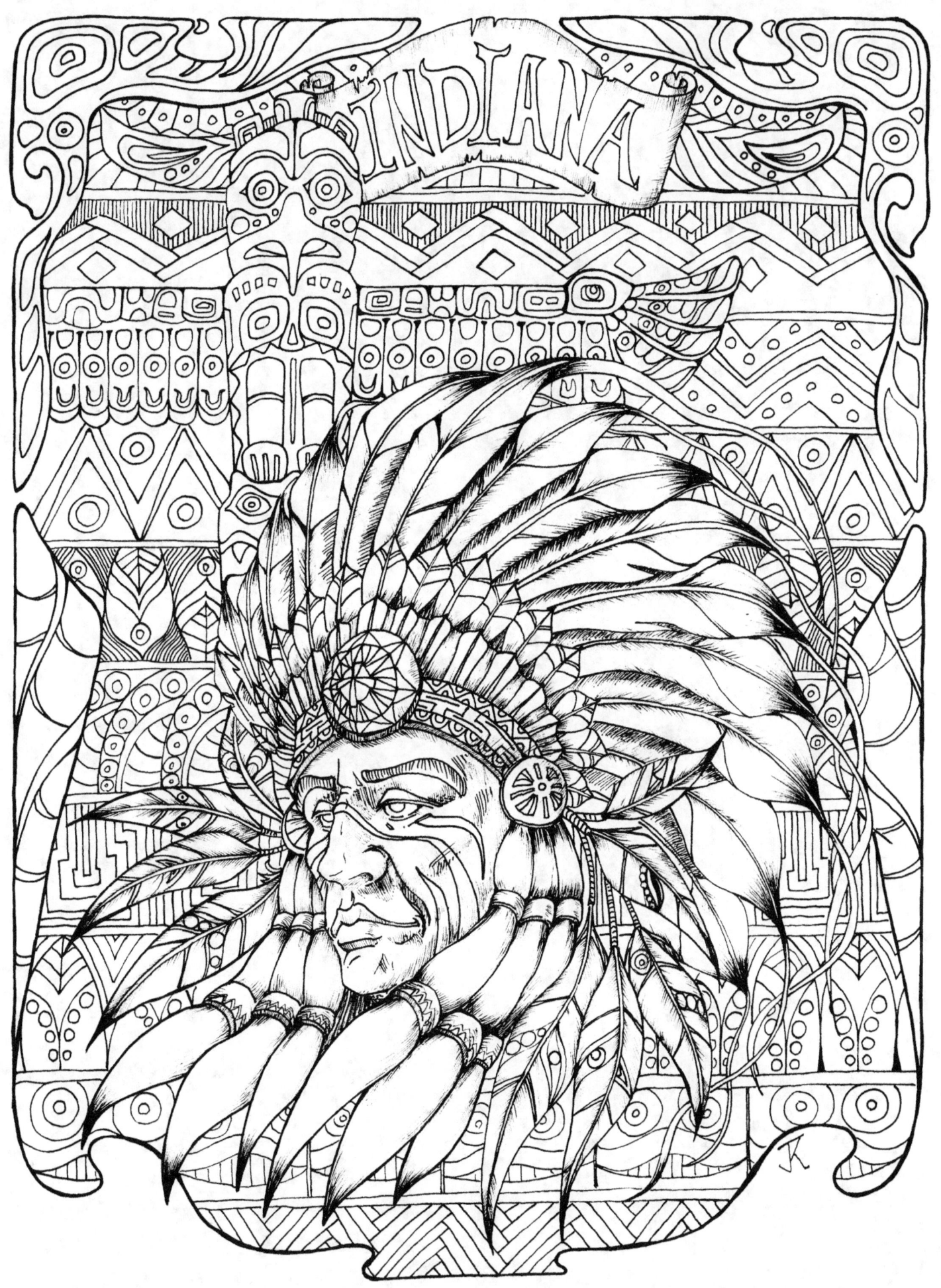

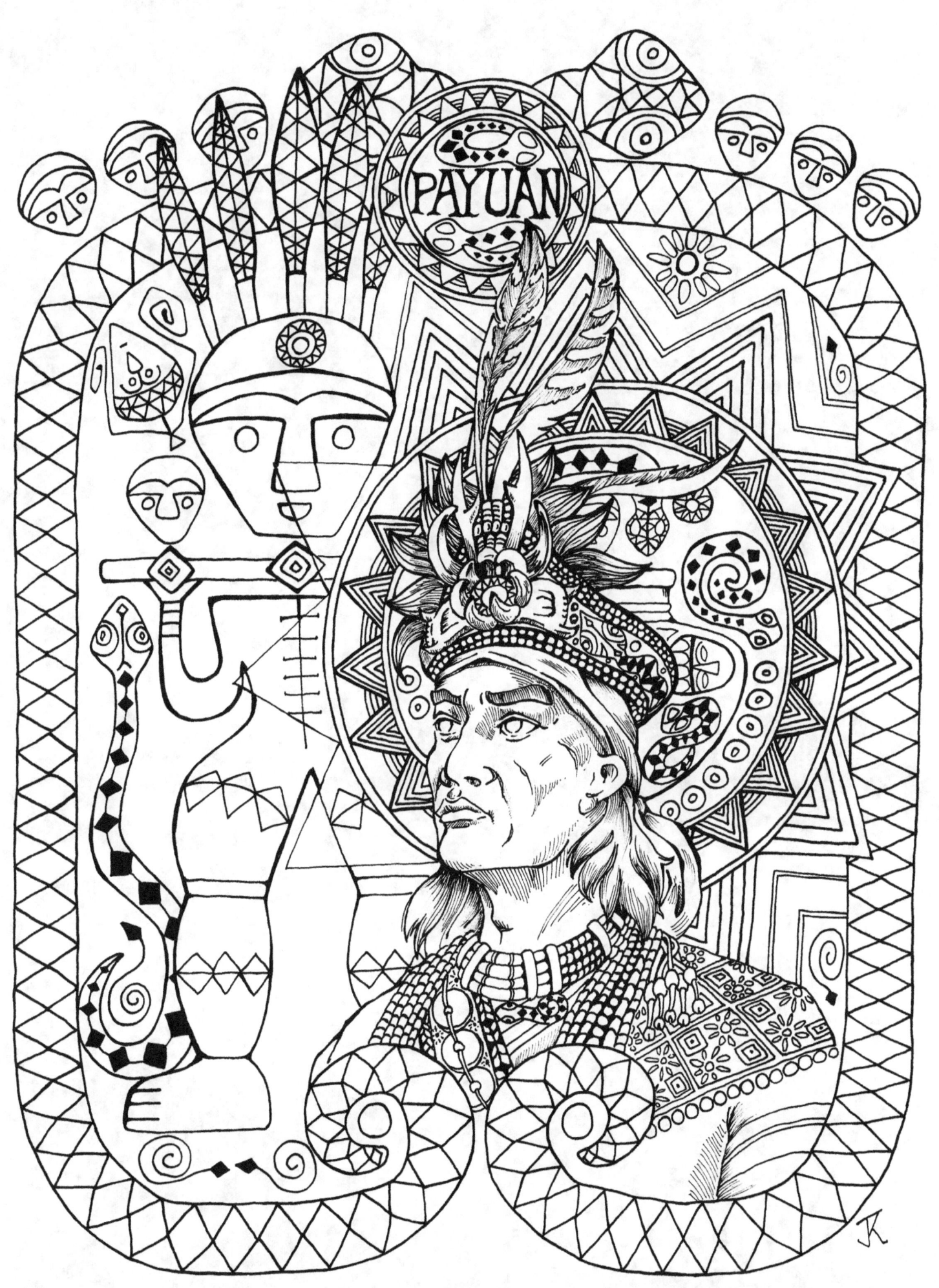

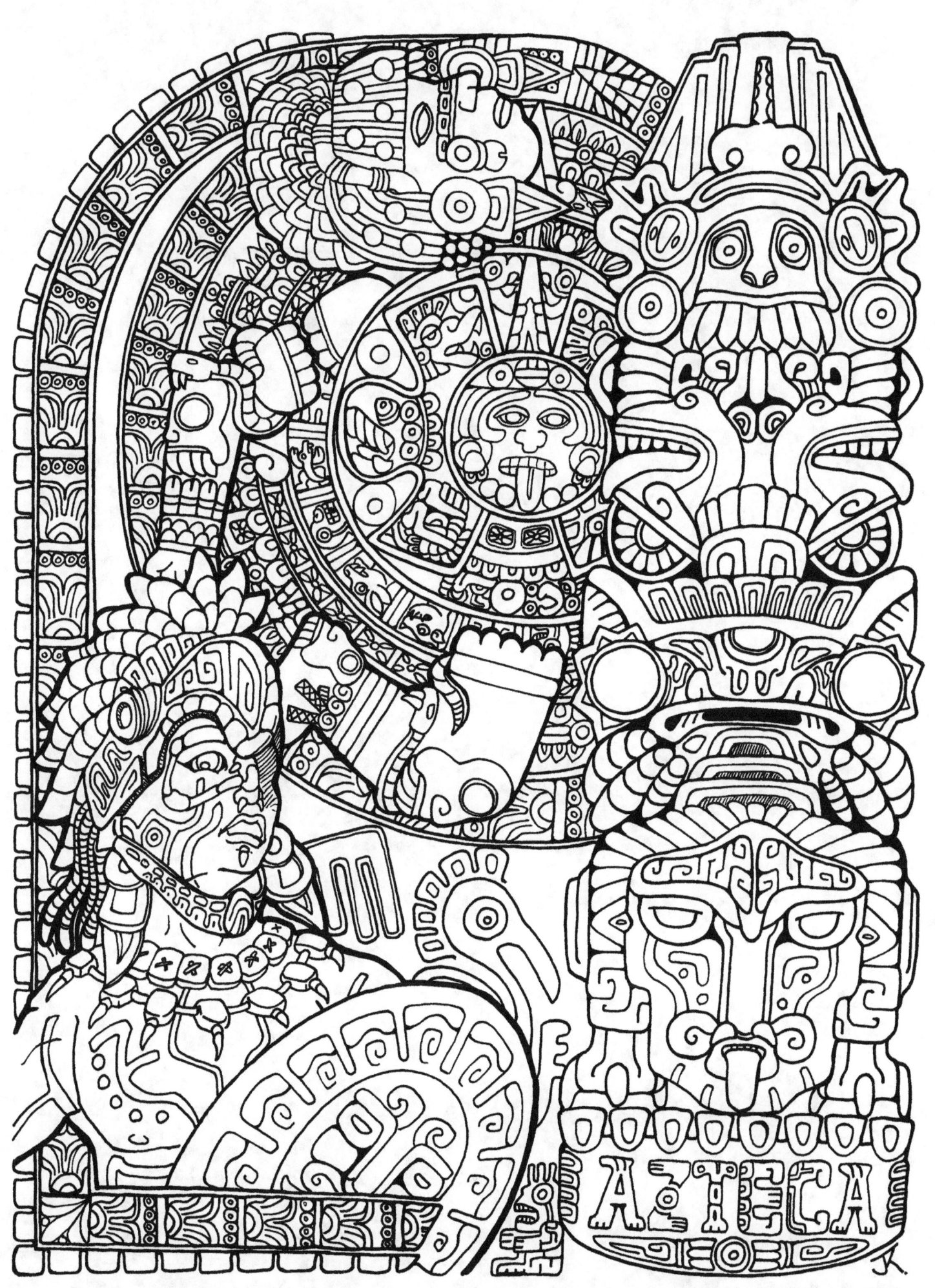

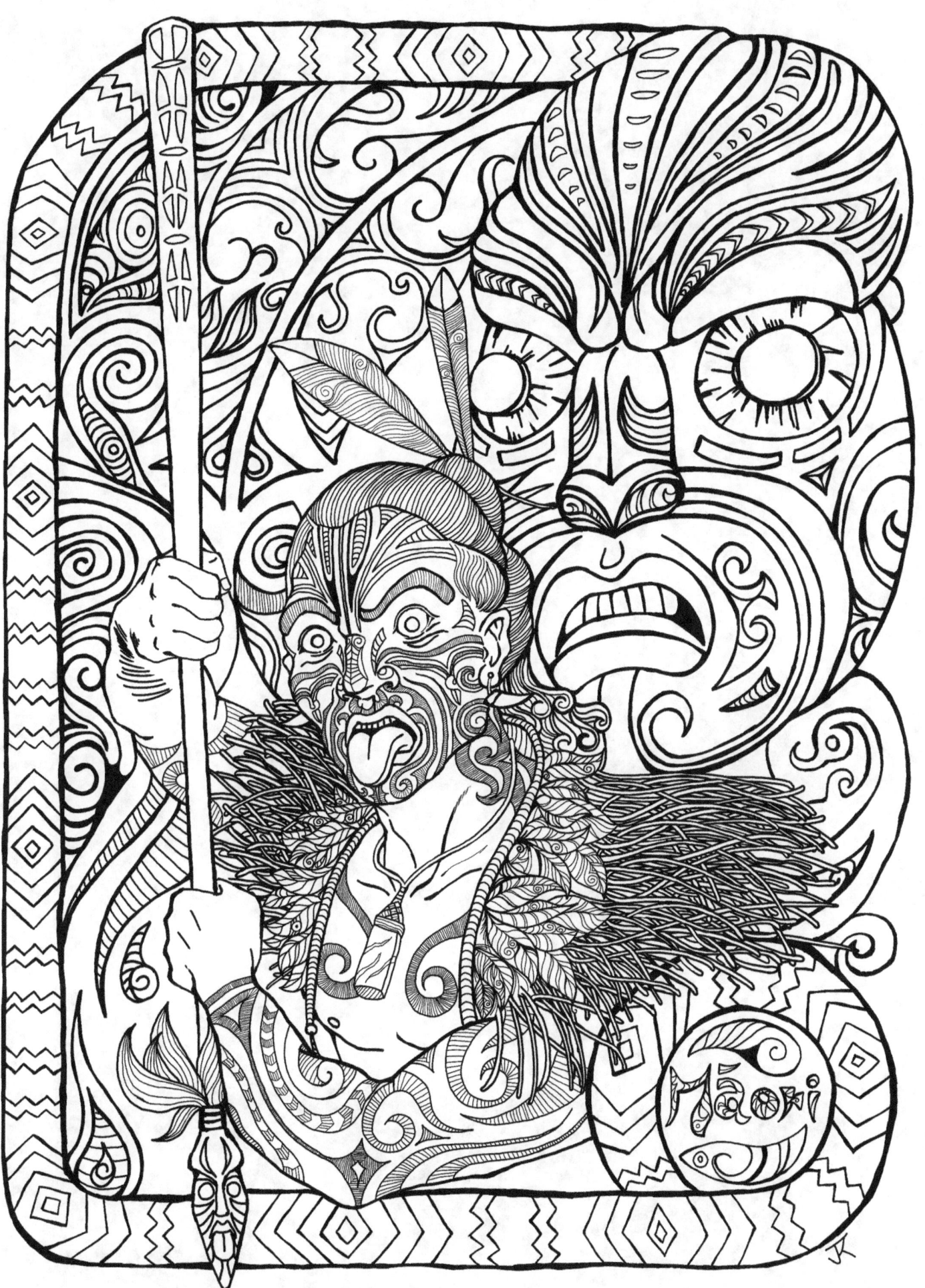

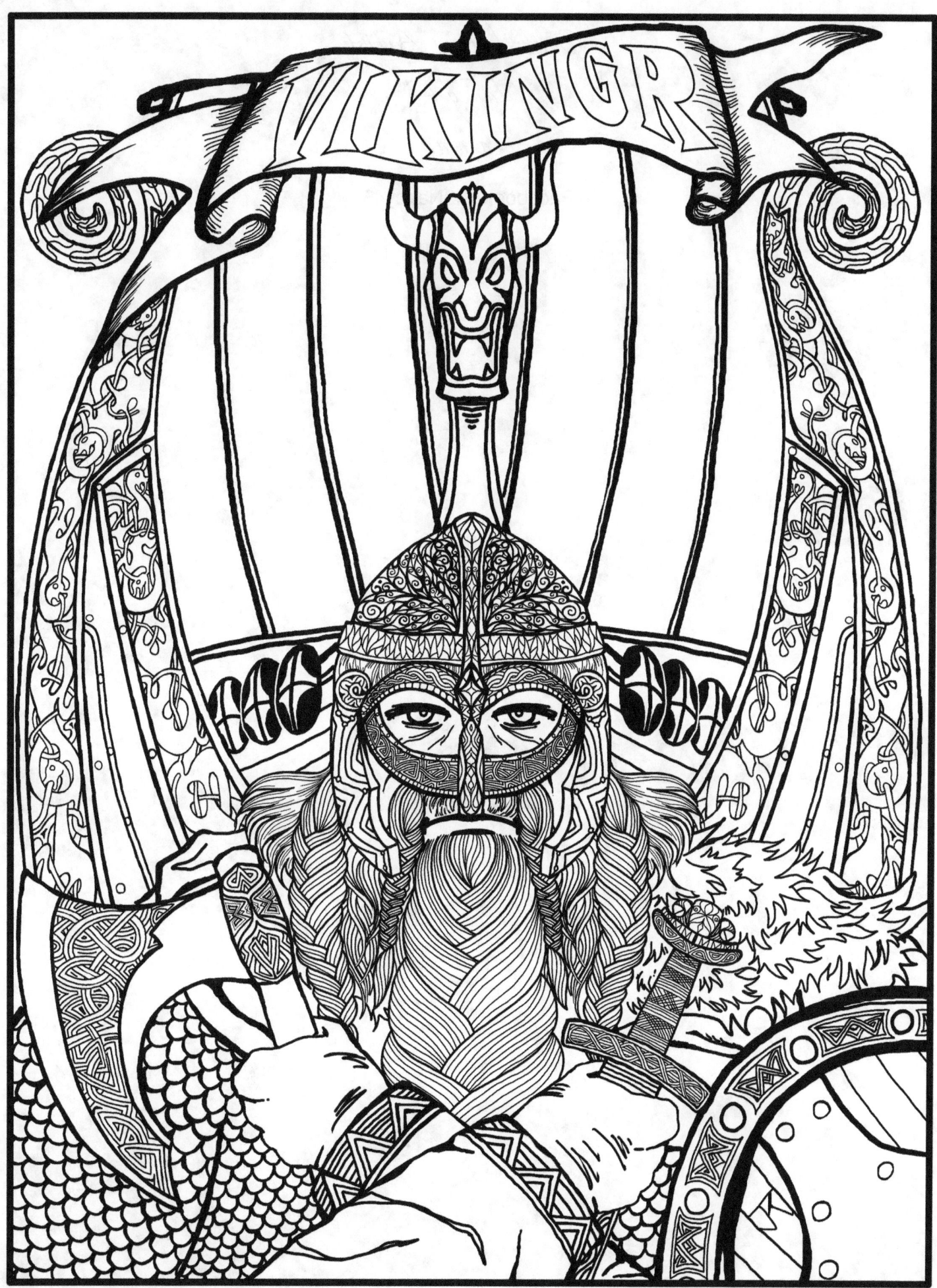

Contributing Artist
Nancy43
Taiwan

Facebook : 43Nancy43

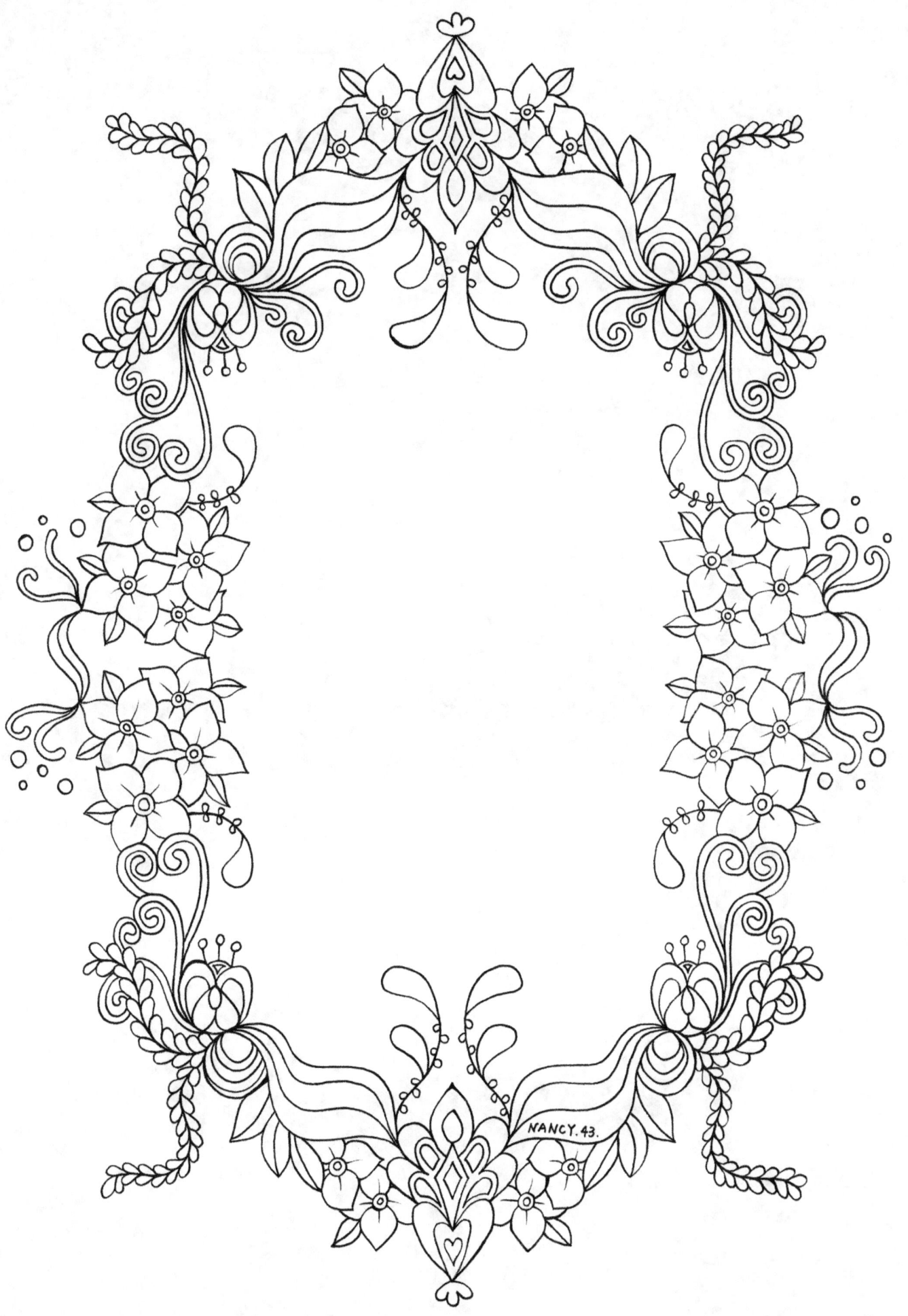

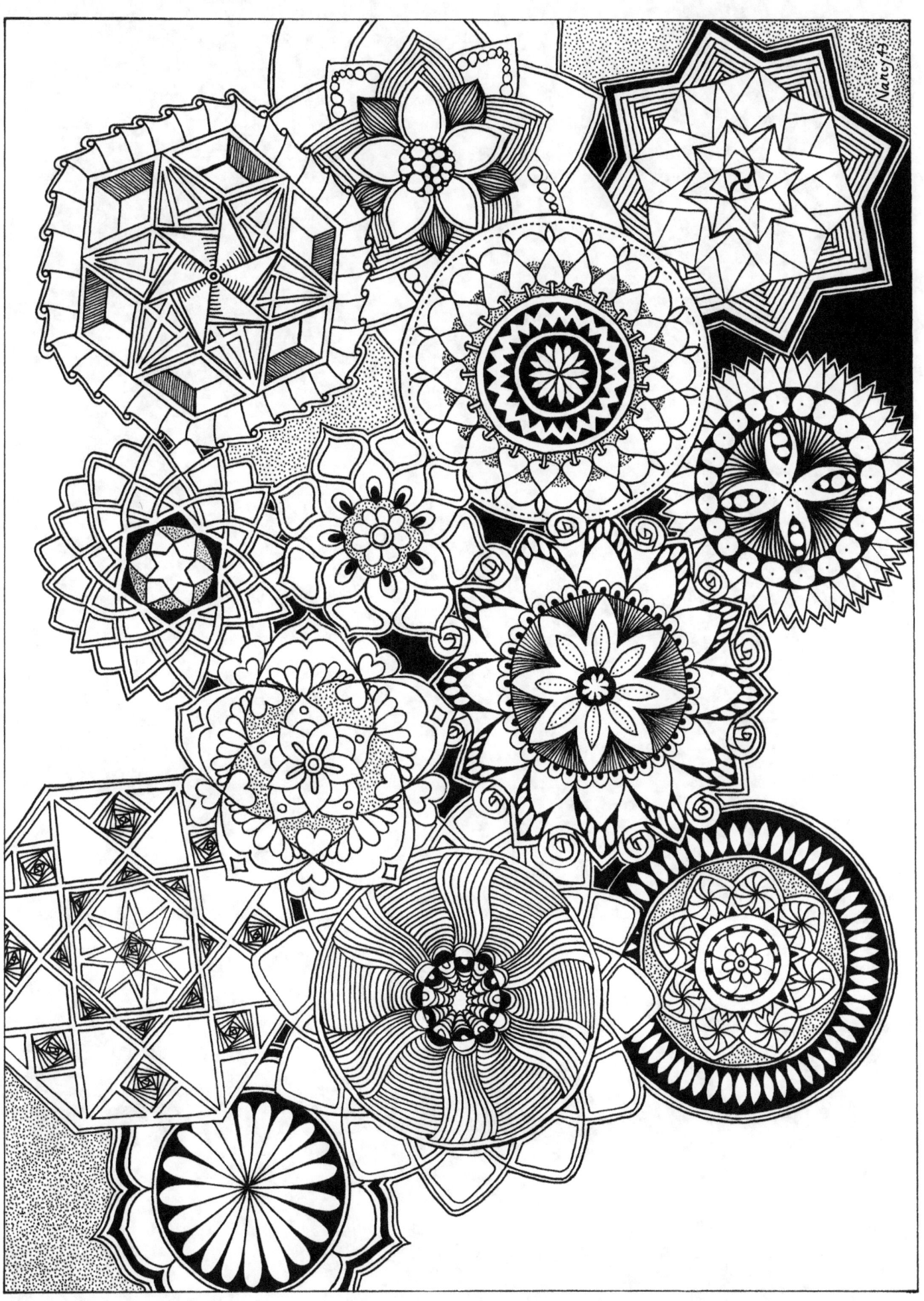

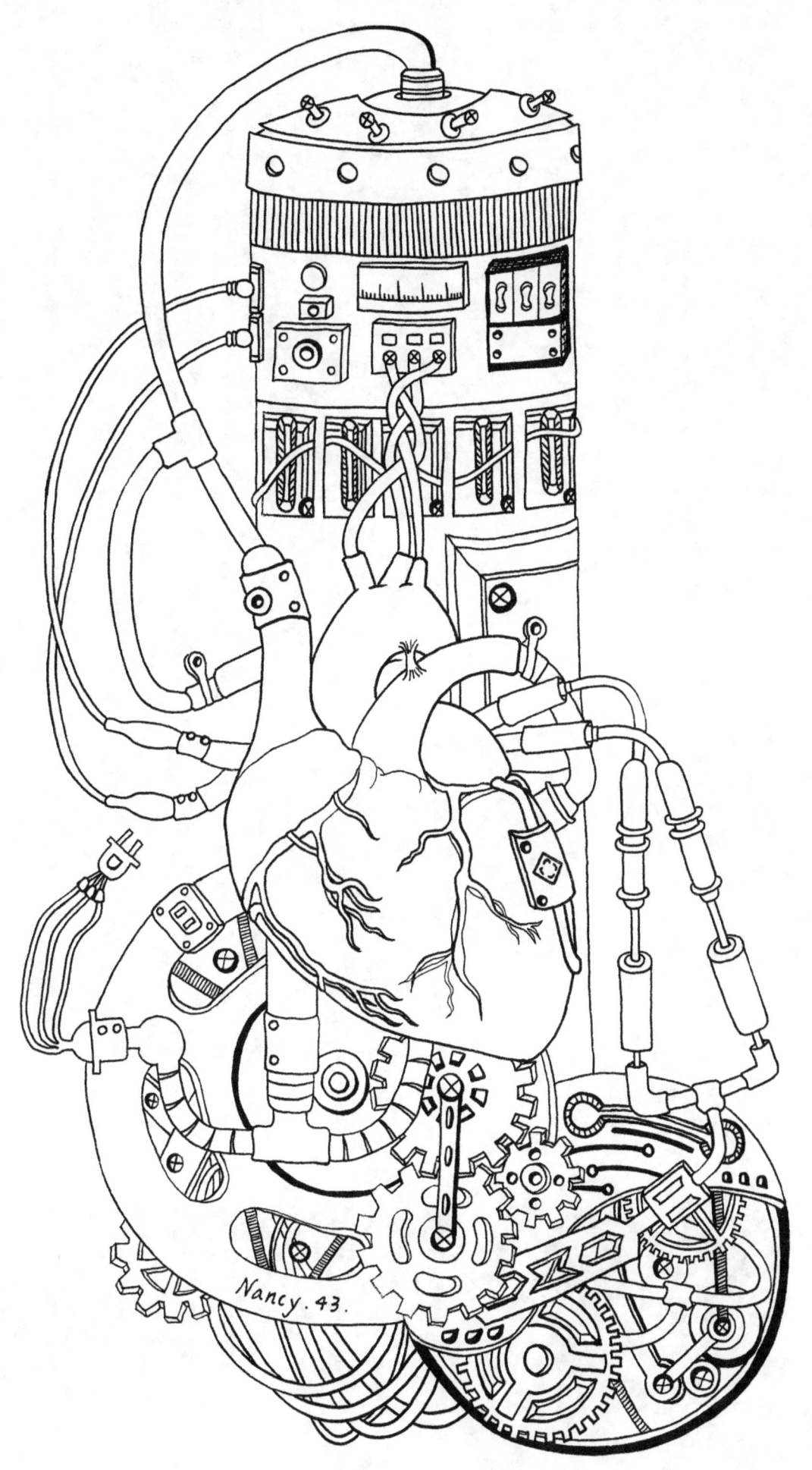

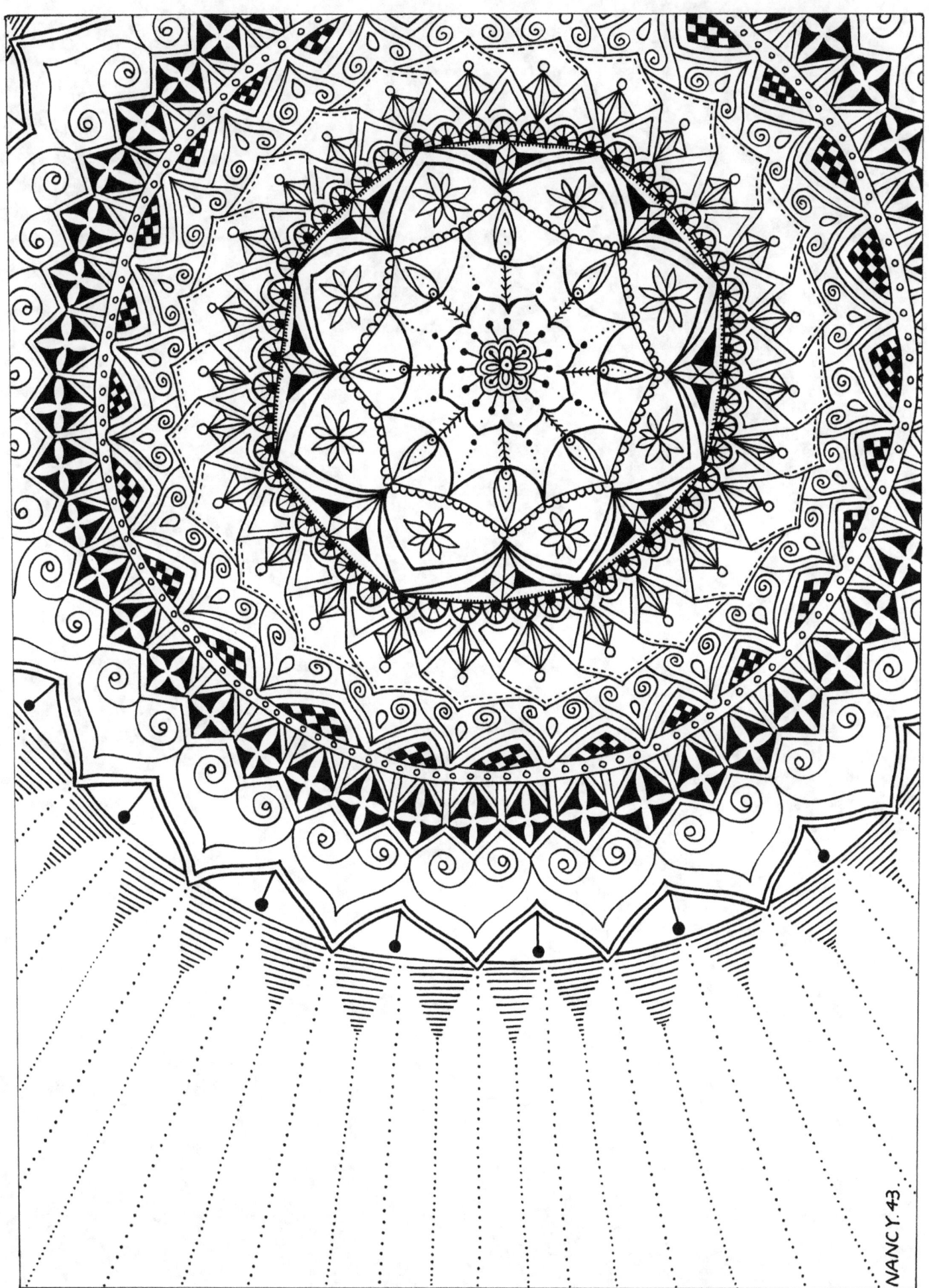

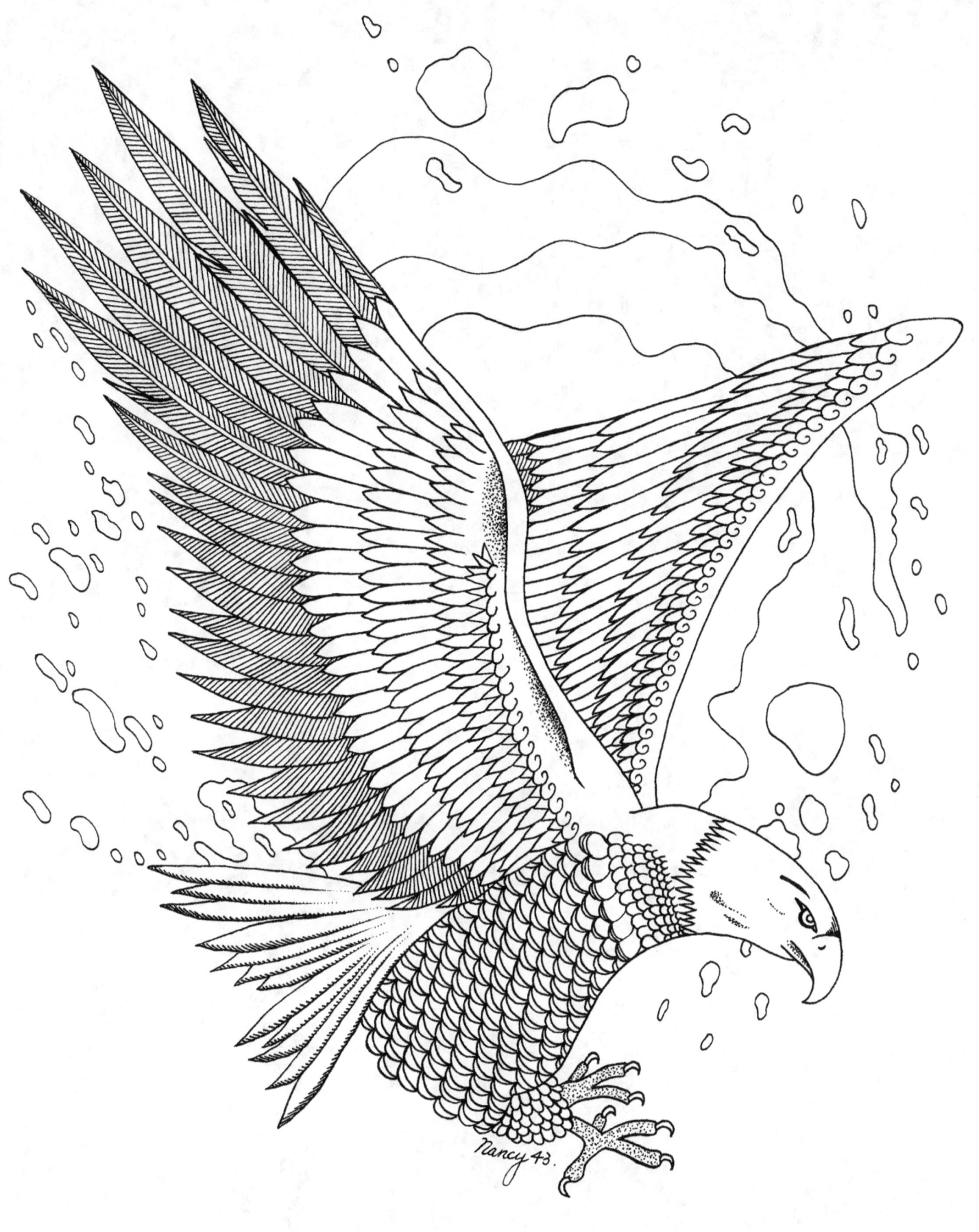

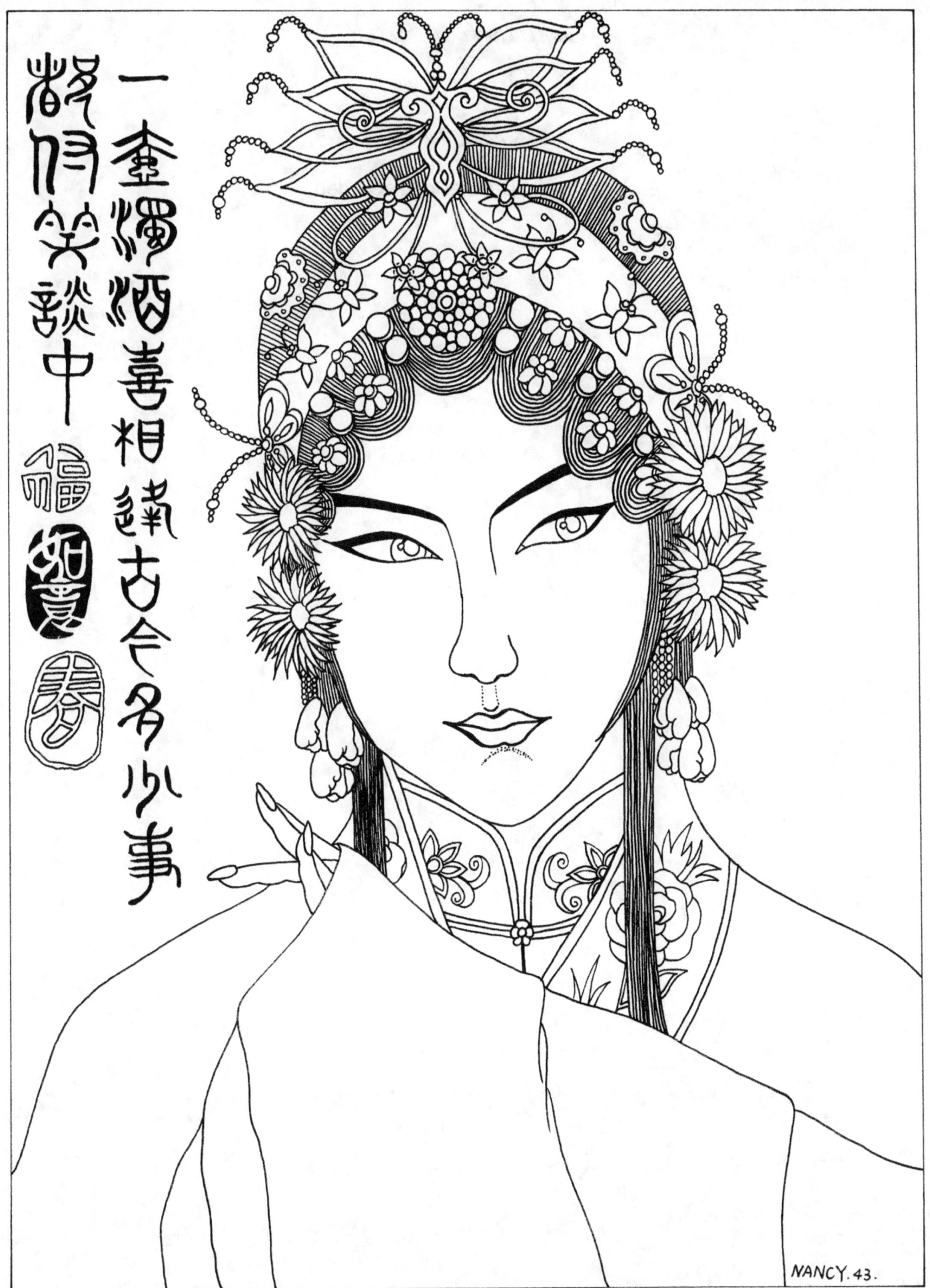

Contributing Artist
Debbie Lai
Taiwan

Facebook : DebbieDoodleGarden

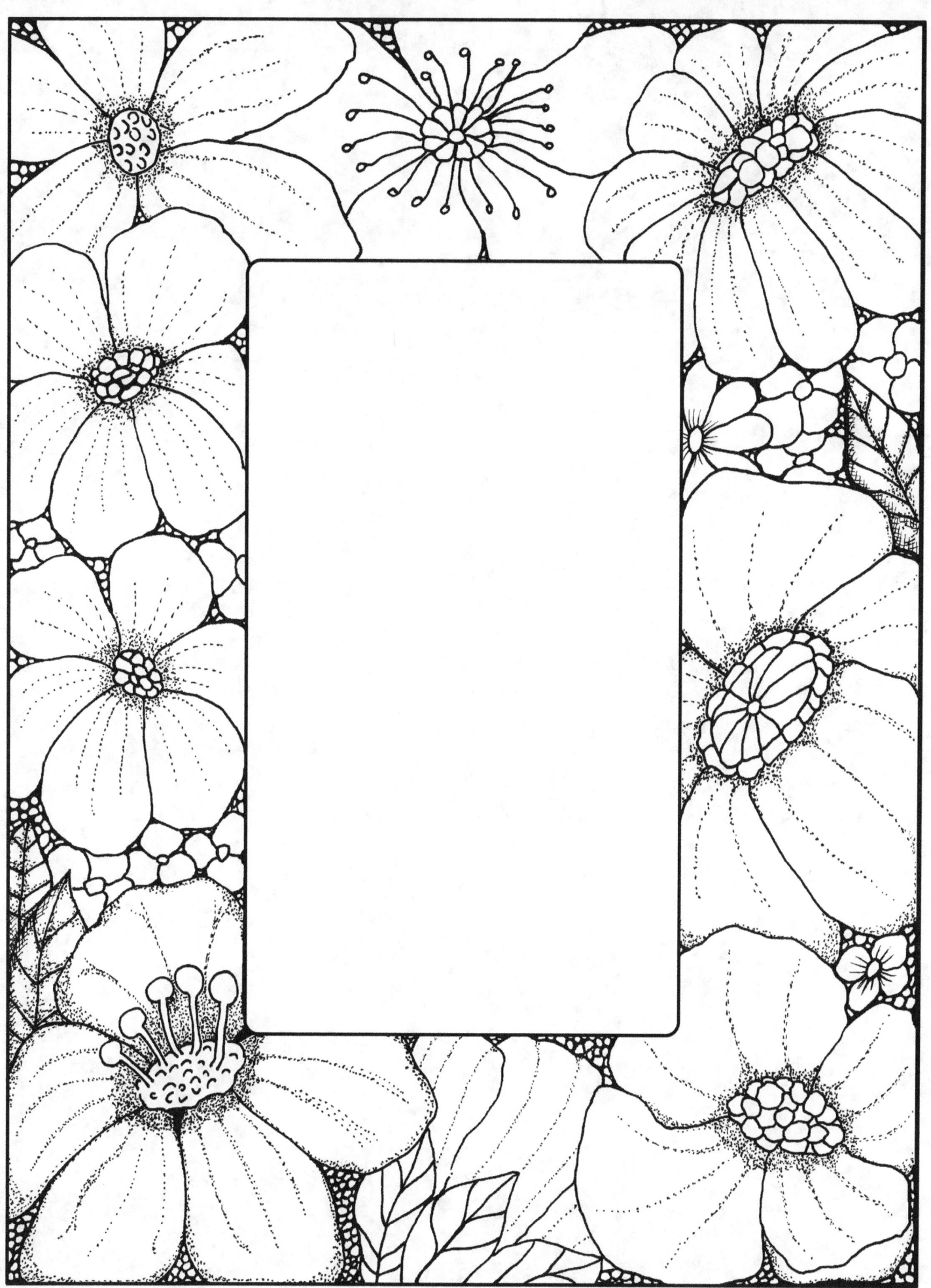

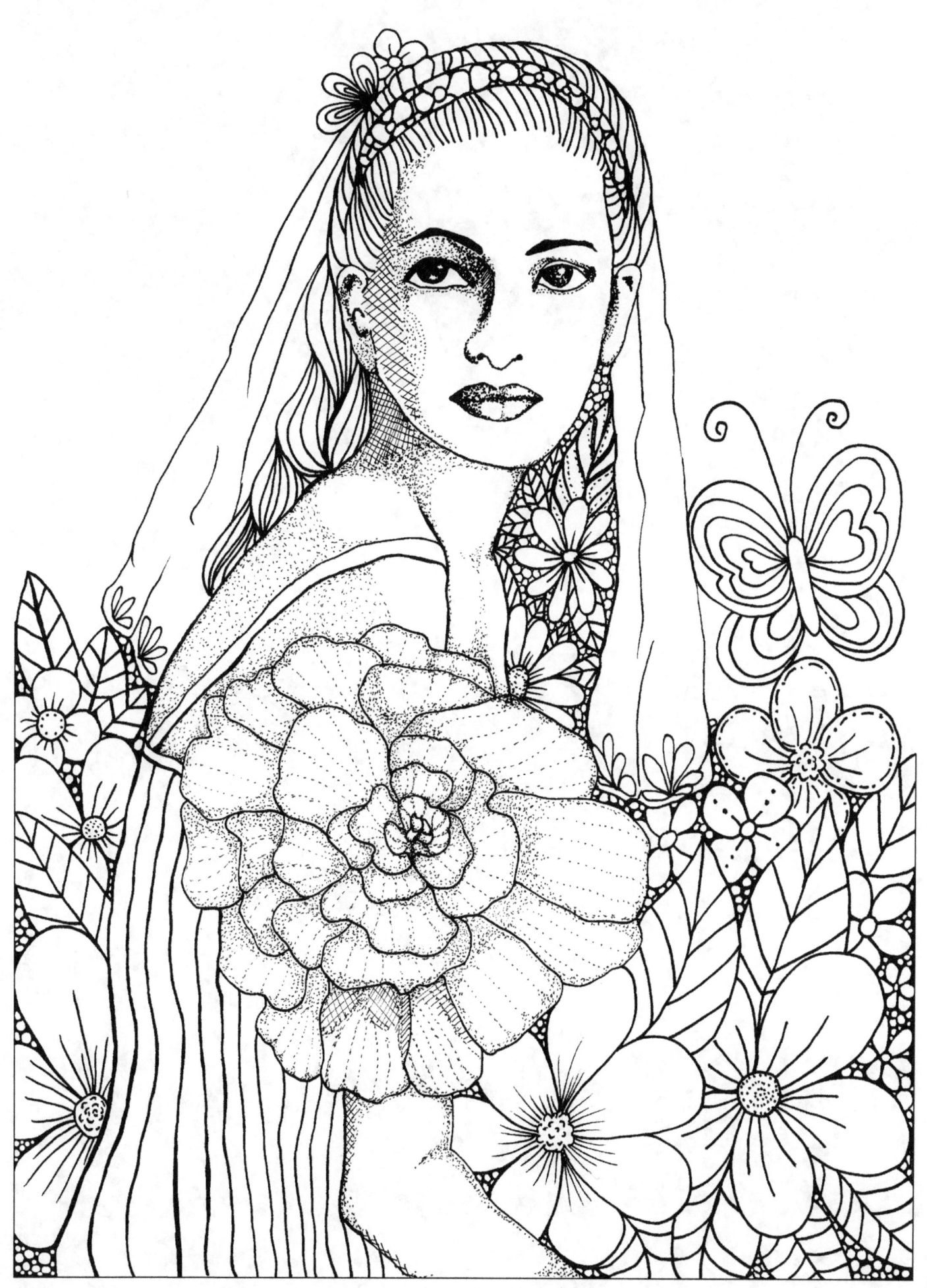

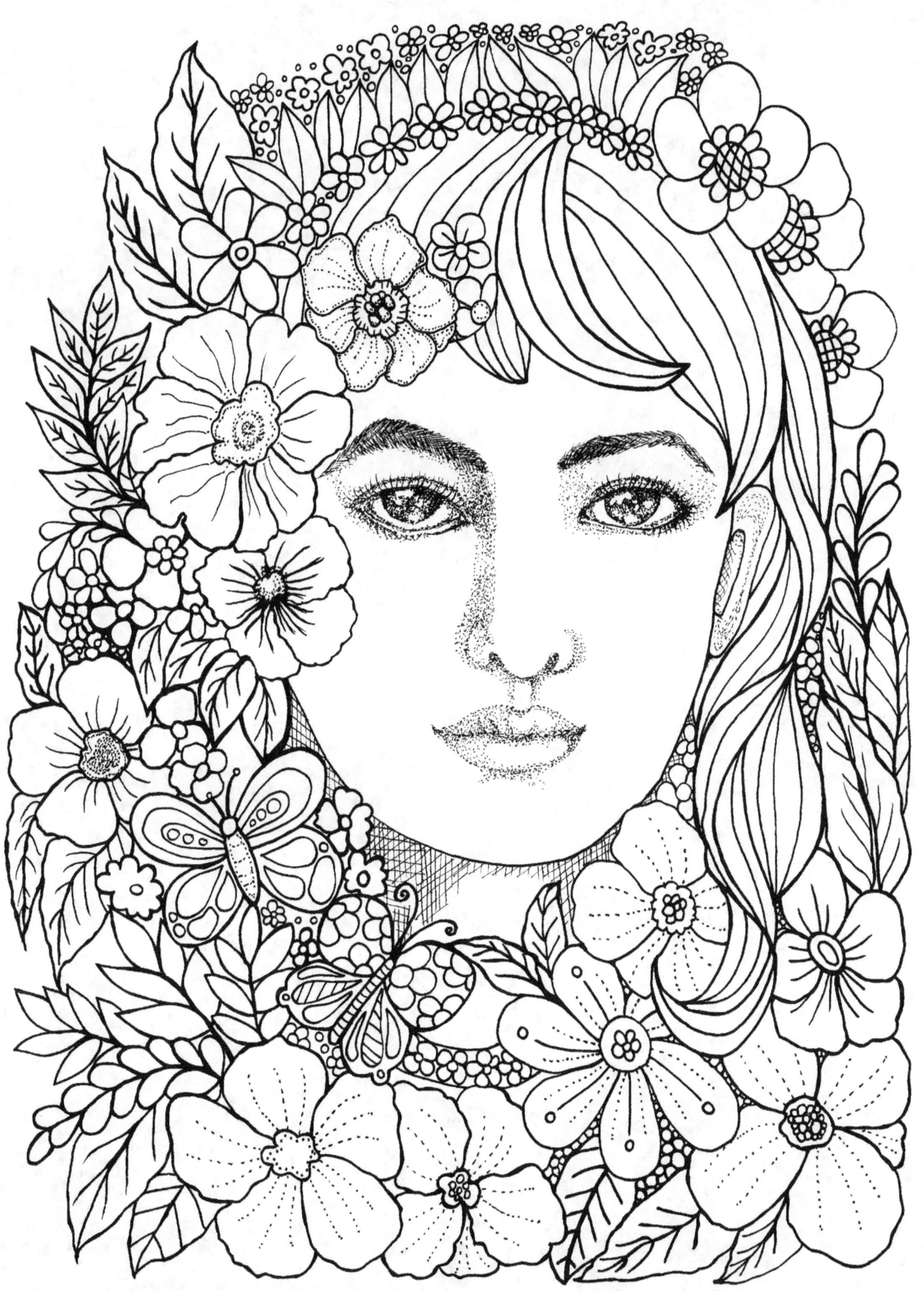

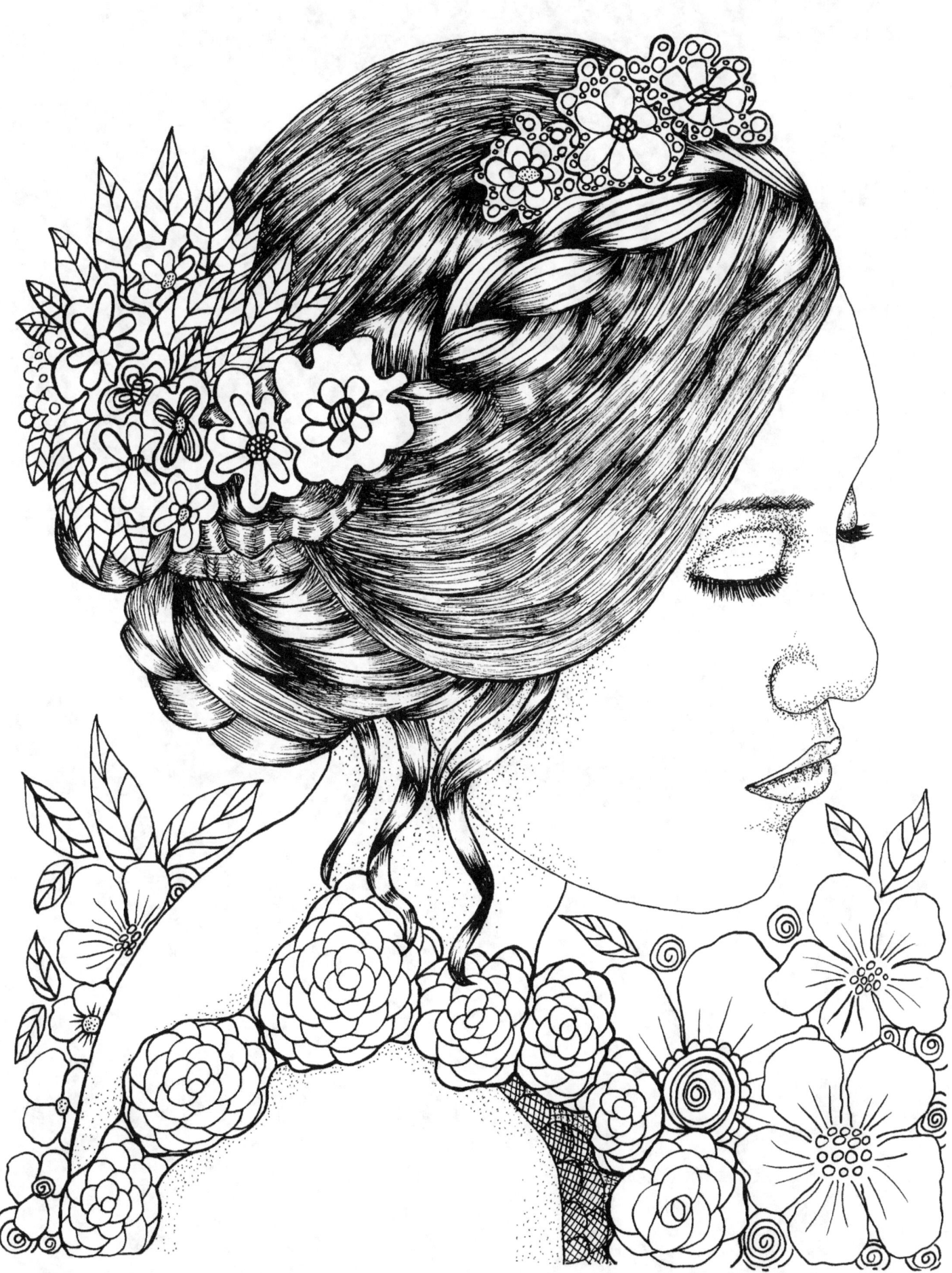

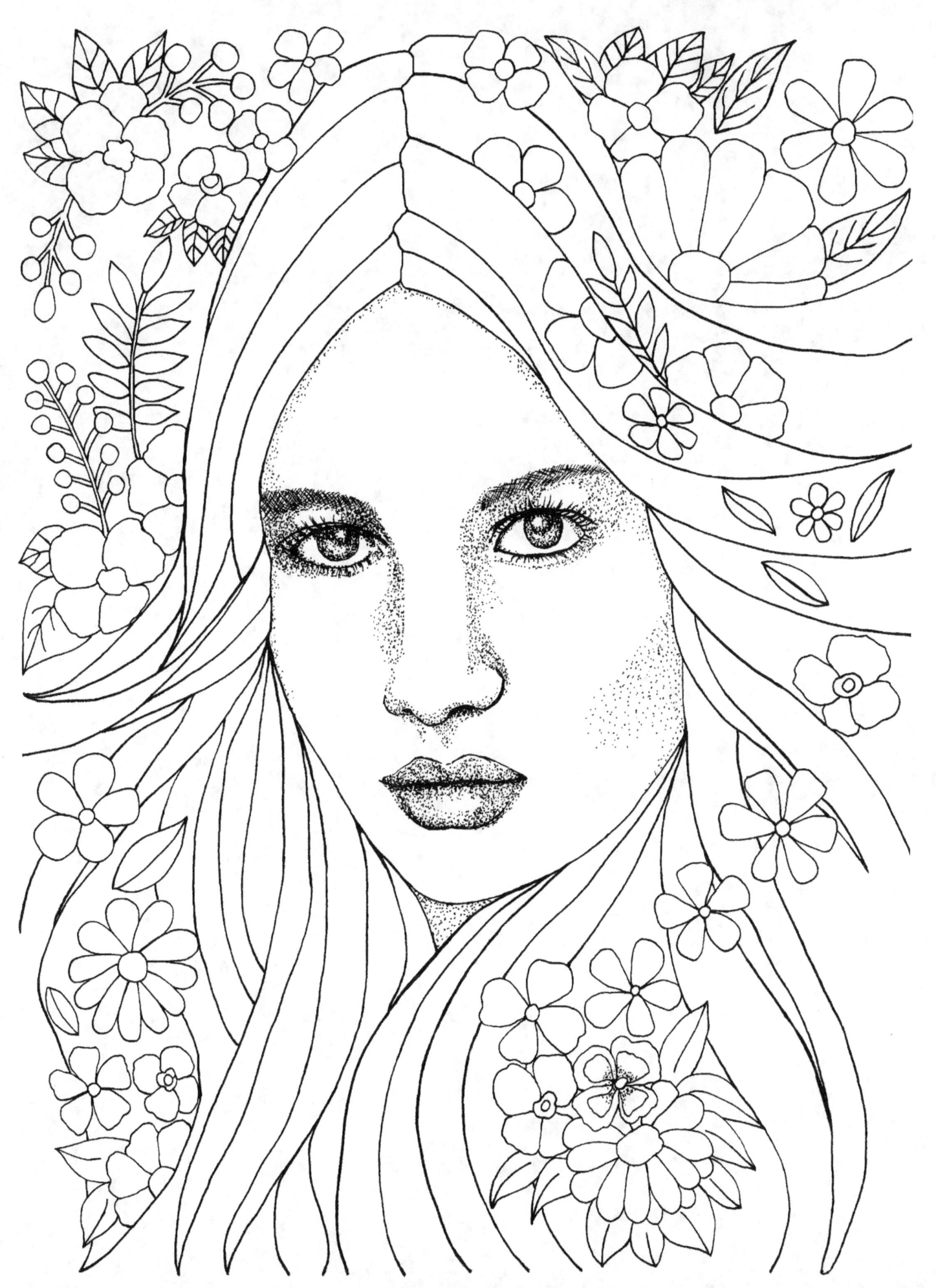

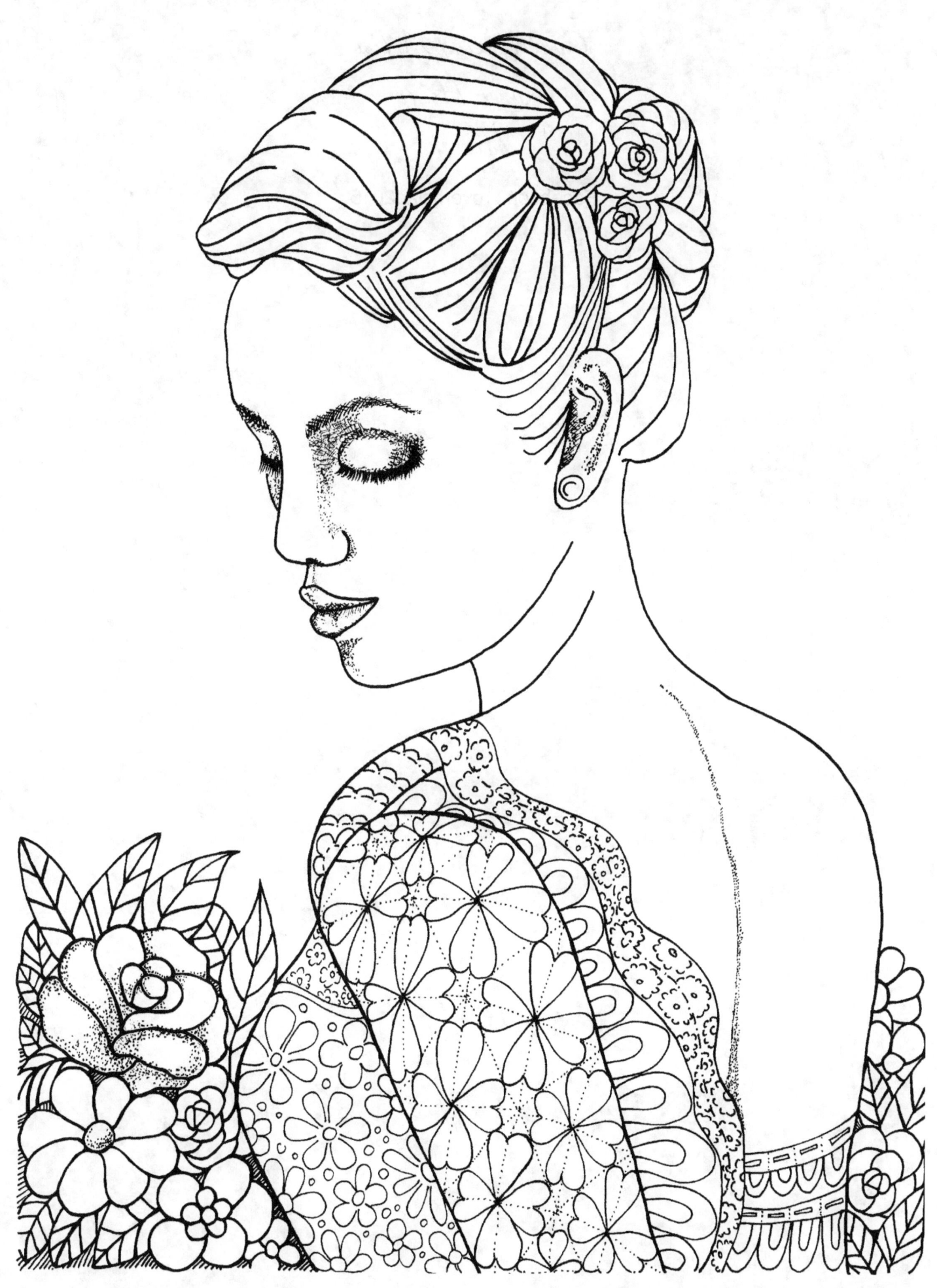

Contributing Artist
Rover Hsiao
Taiwan

Facebook : roverhsiao2015

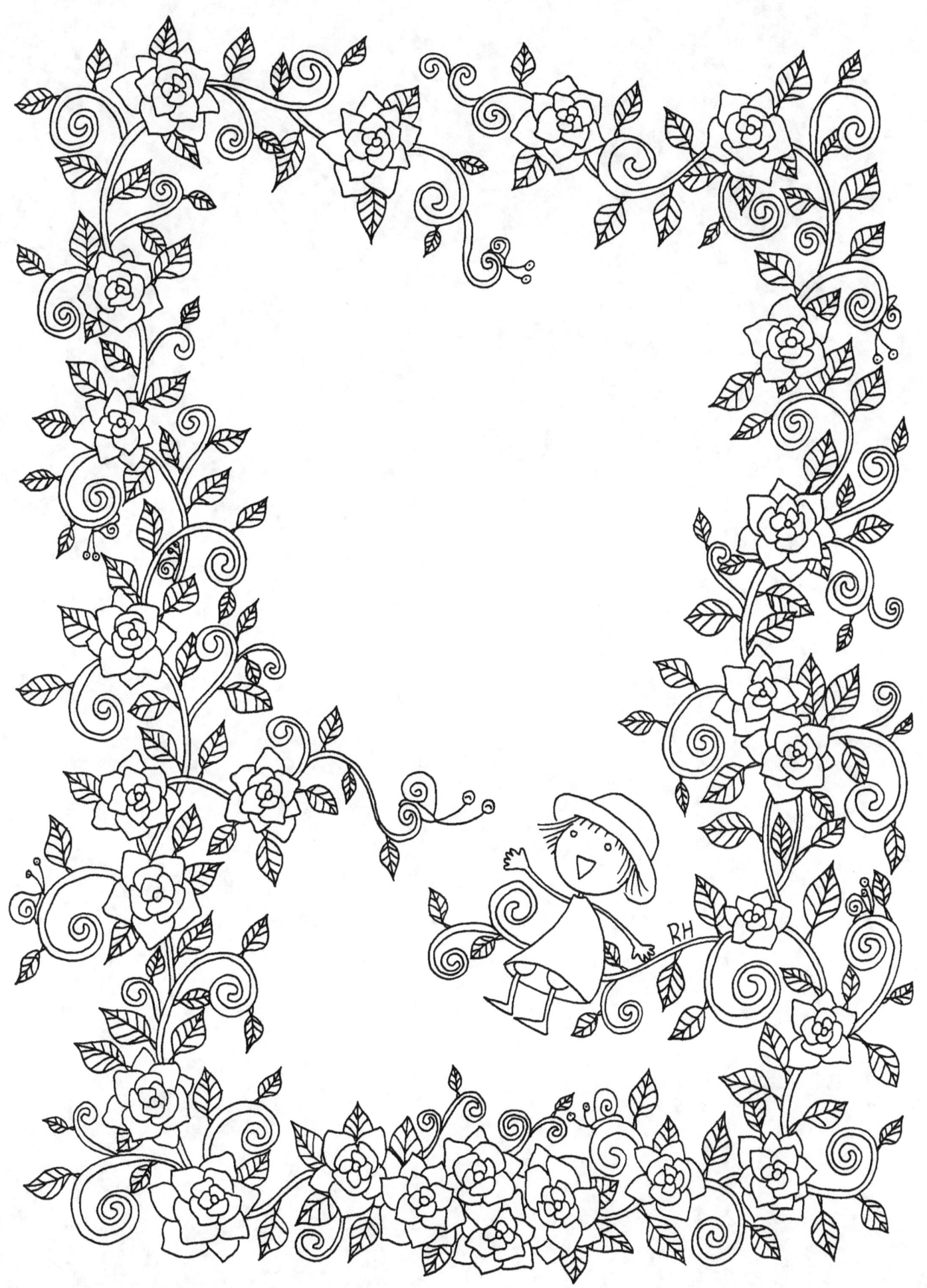

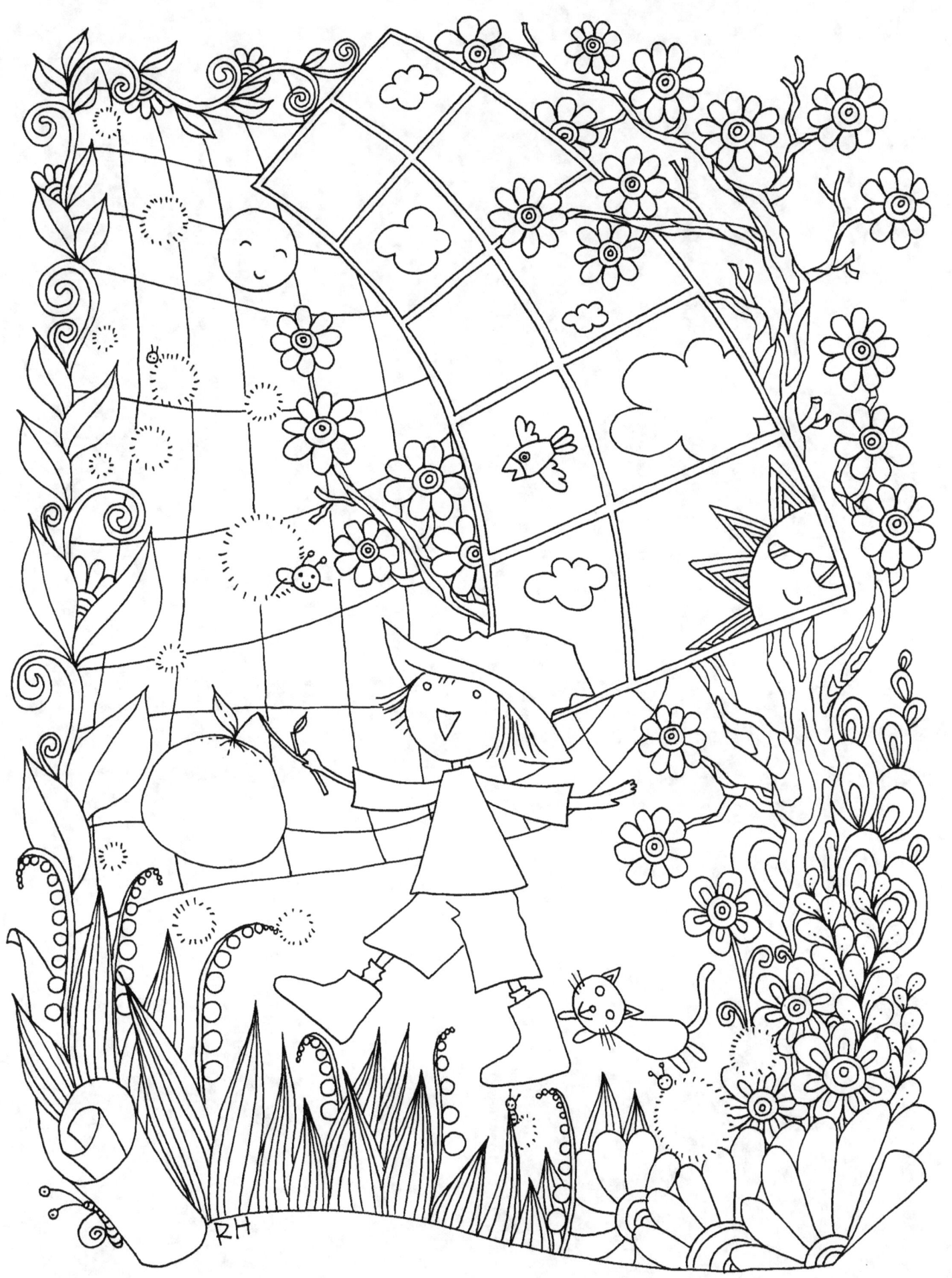

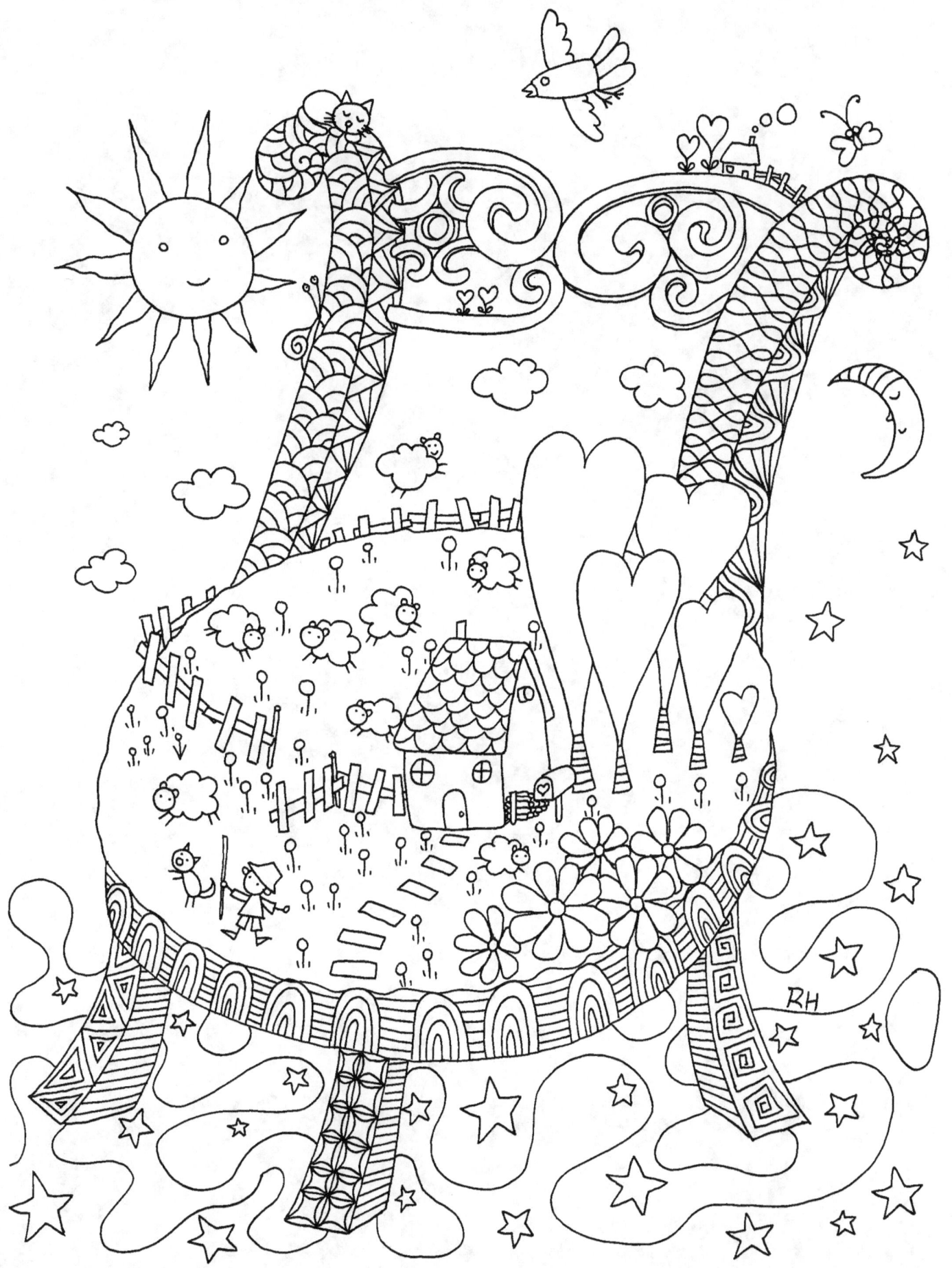

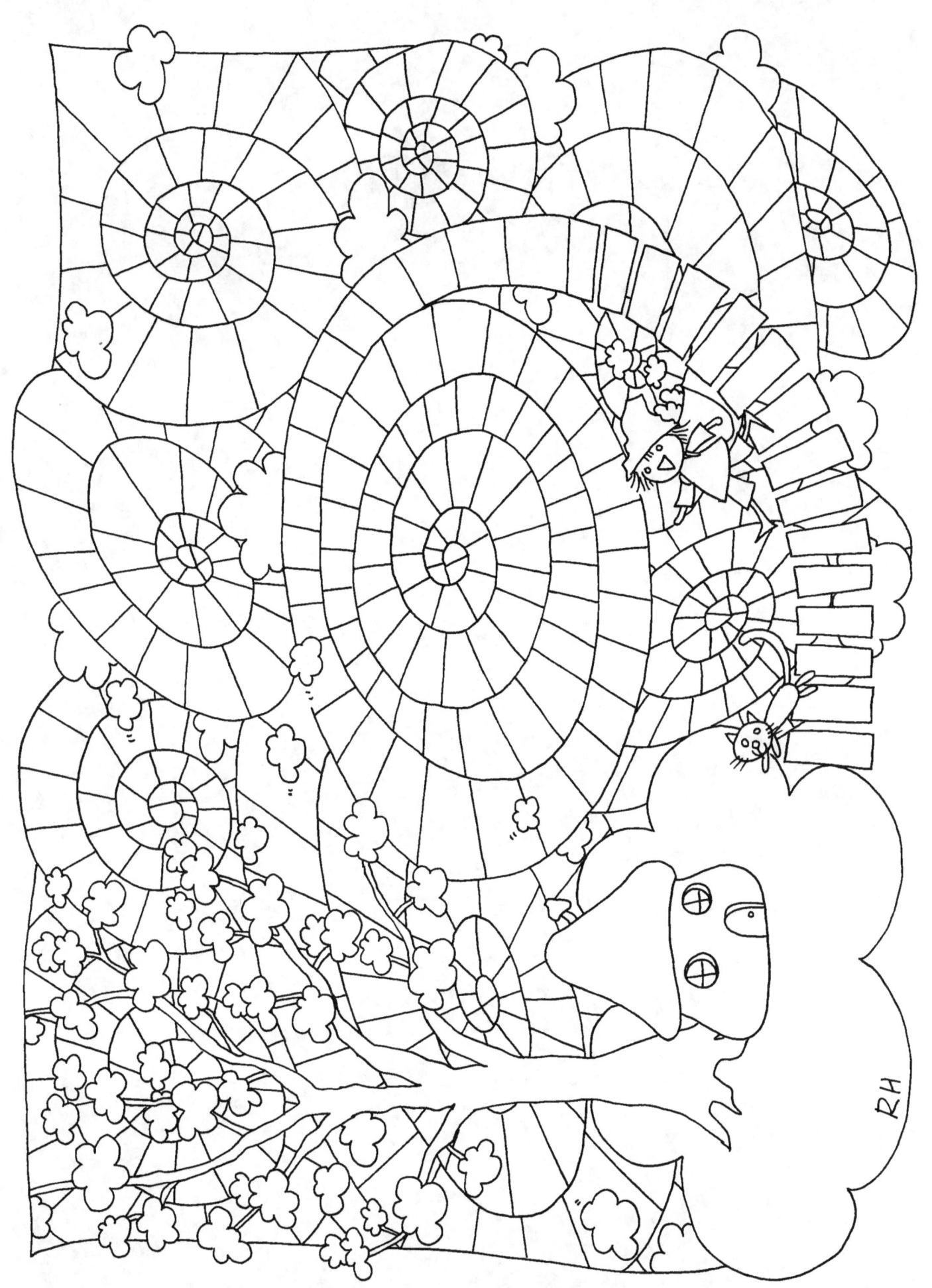

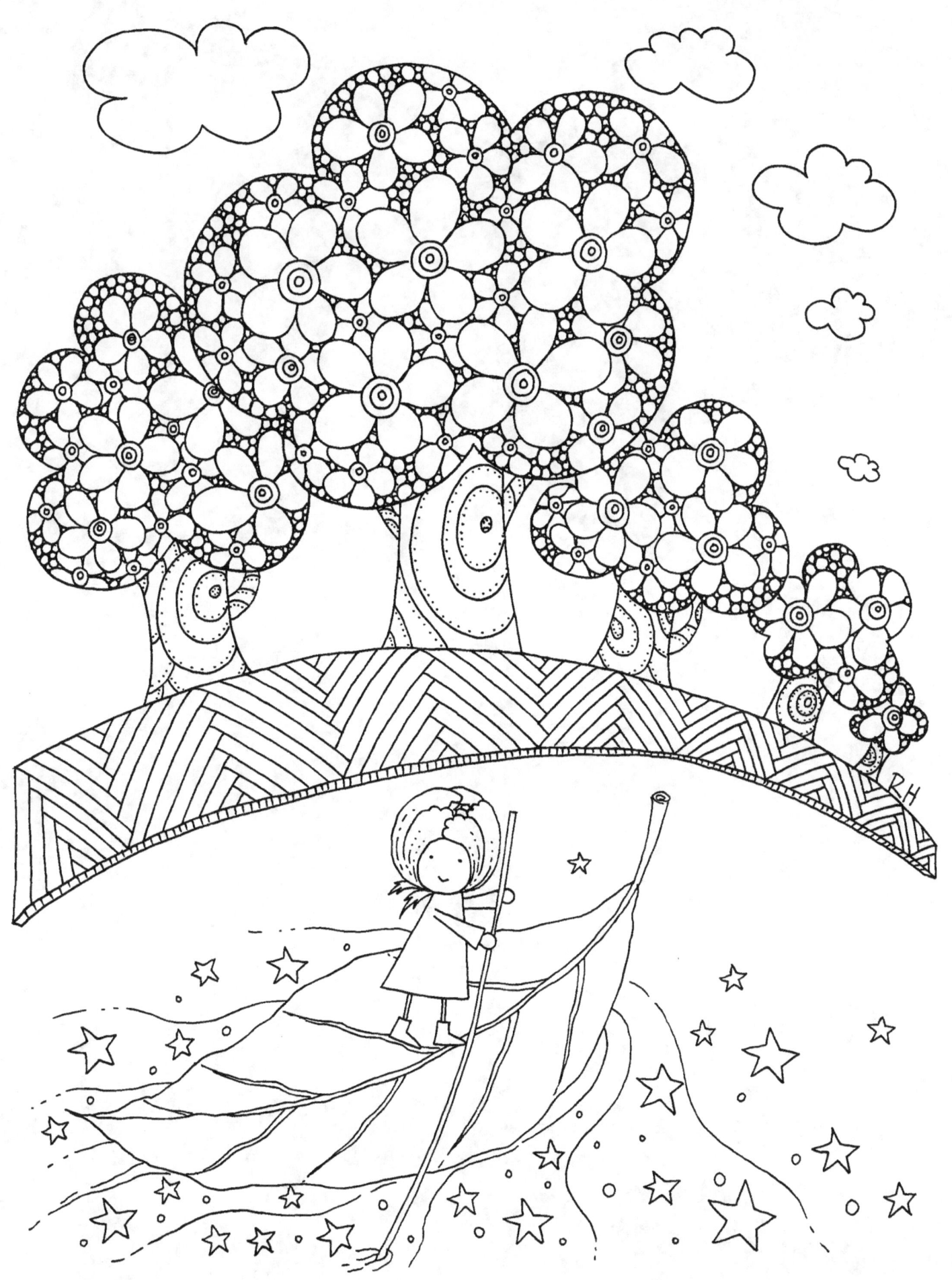

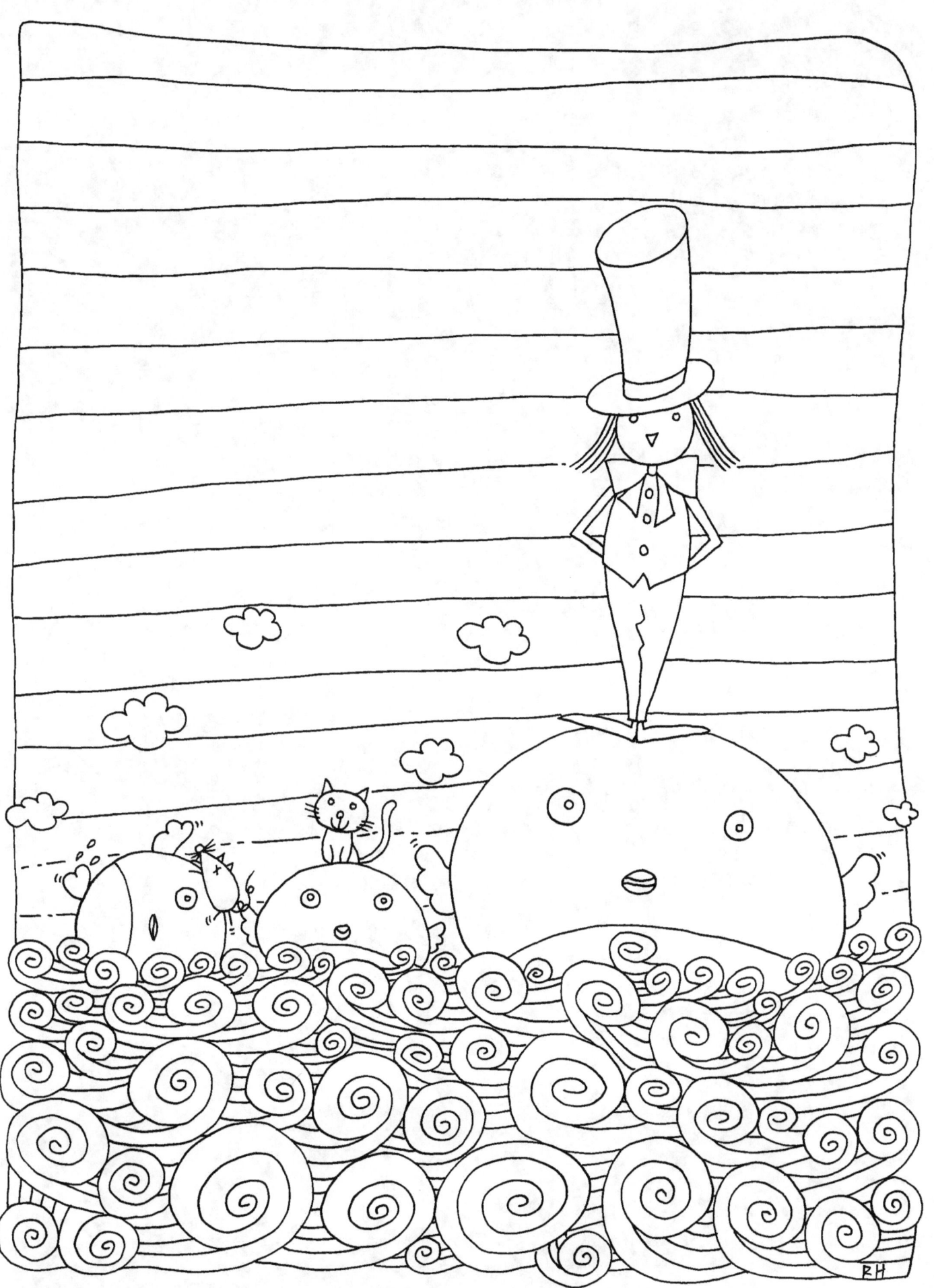

Test your colors here on the samples from
"My Pocket Coloring Companion"
&
"My Coloring Companion"

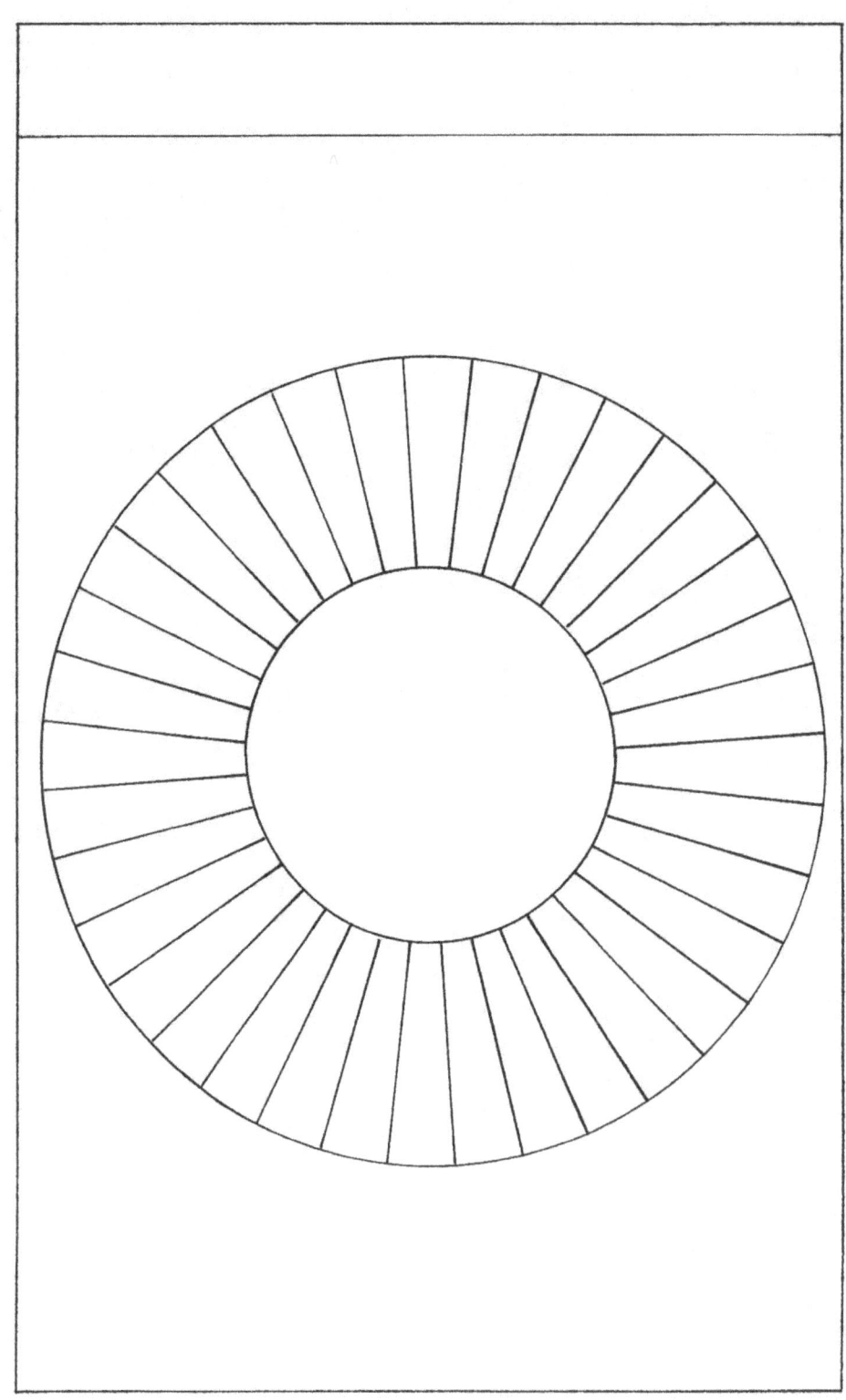

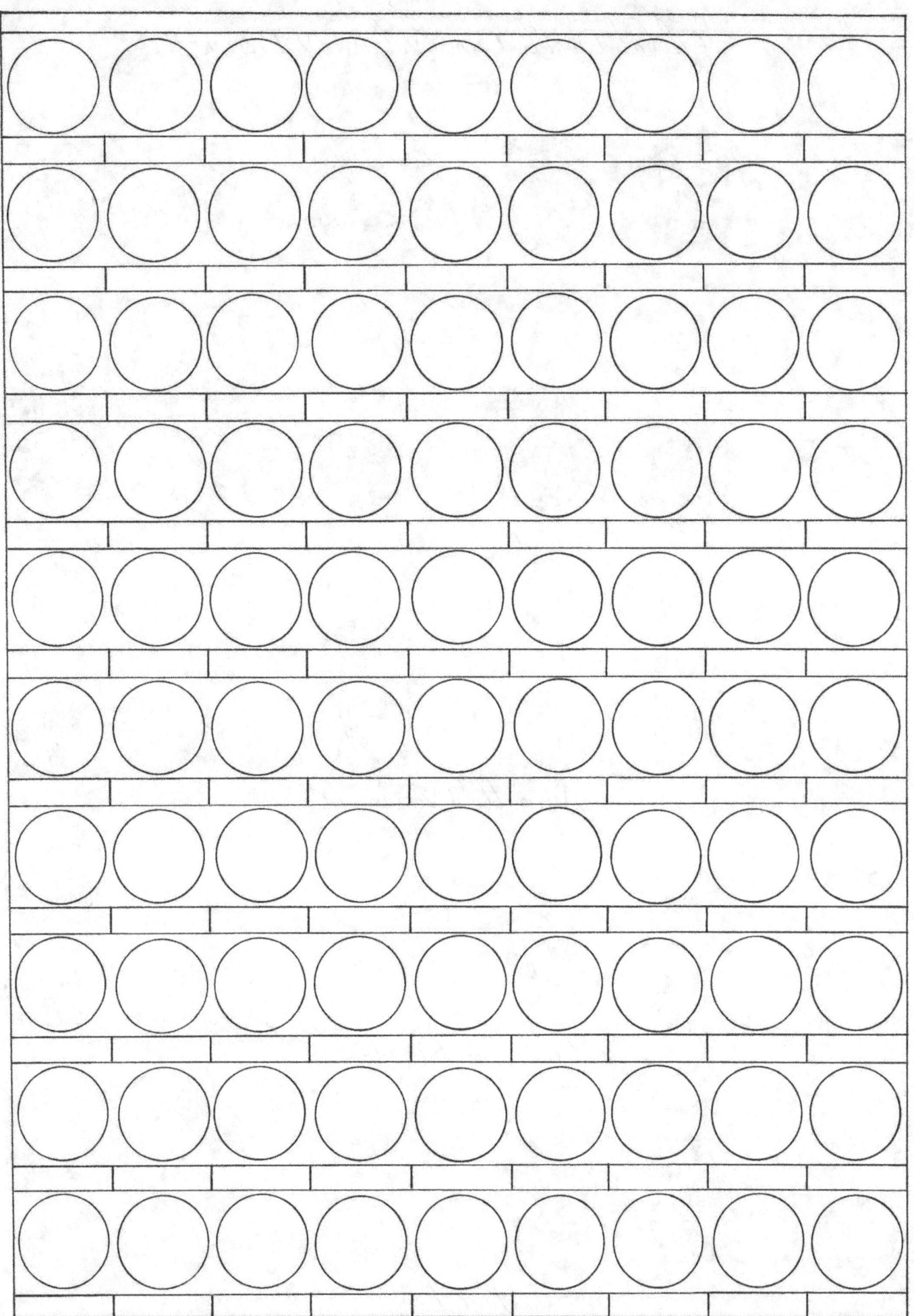

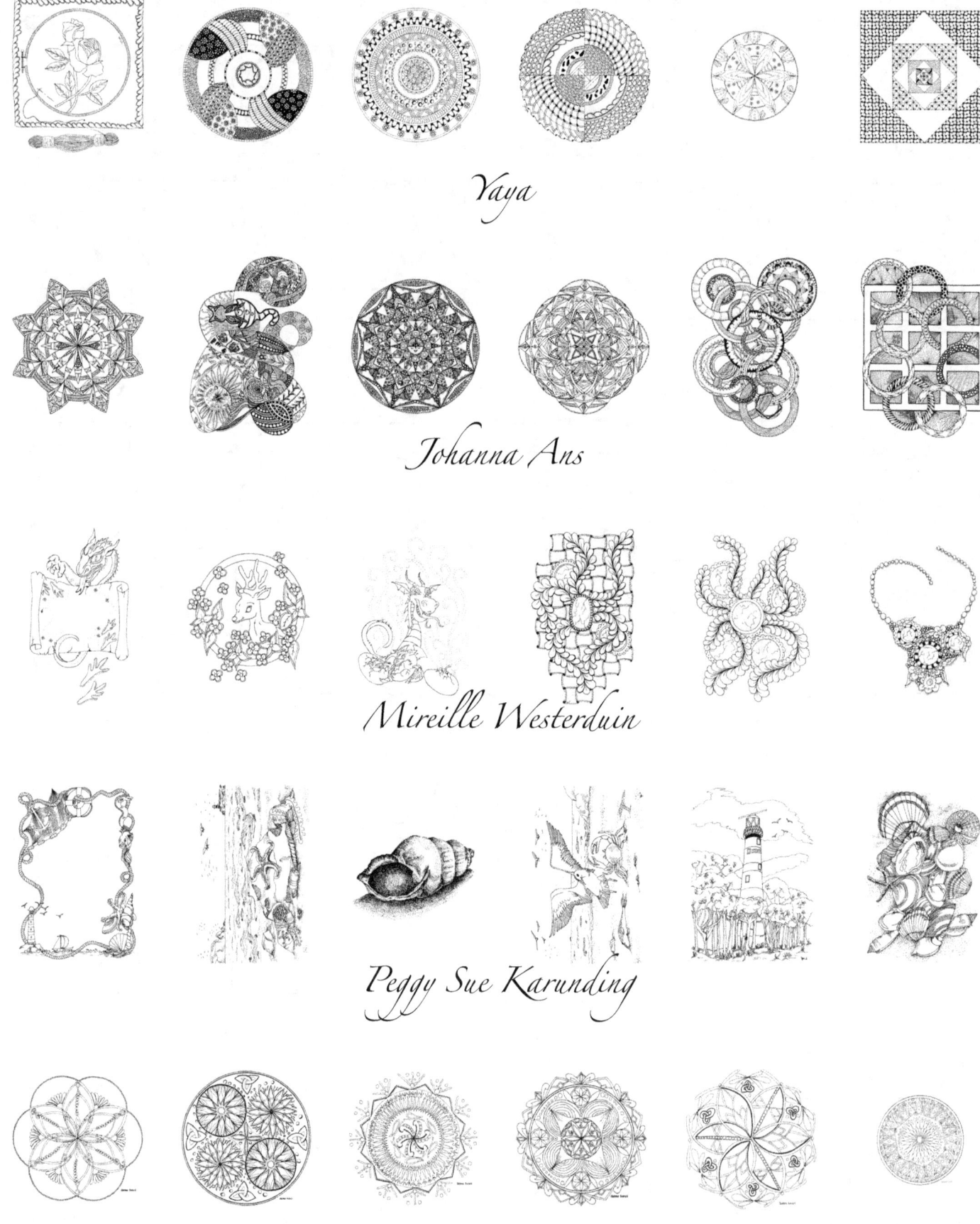

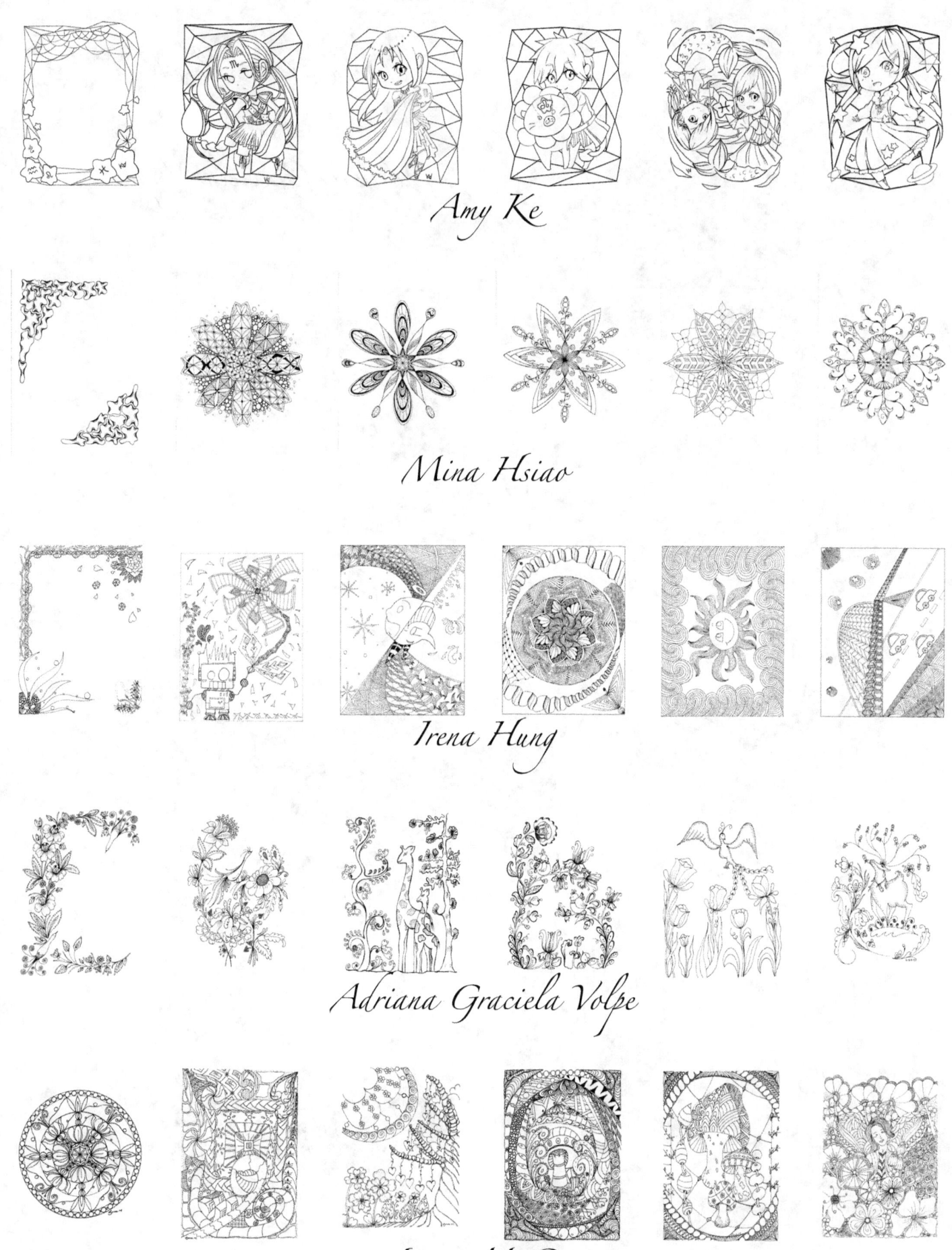

Amy Ke

Mina Hsiao

Irena Hung

Adriana Graciela Volpe

Lynne McGee

Drawn & colored by
Adriana Graciela Volpe